The Enquiring University

Compliance and contestation in higher education

Stephen Rowland

Society for Research into Higher Education
& Open University Press

Open University Press
McGraw-Hill Education
McGraw-Hill House
Shoppenhangers Road
Maidenhead
Berkshire
England
SL6 2QL

email: enquiries@openup.co.uk
world wide web: www.openup.co.uk

and Two Penn Plaza, New York, NY 10121–2289, USA

First published 2006

Reprinted 2007

Copyright © Stephen Rowland 2006

A catalogue record of this book is available from the British Library

ISBN-10: 0 335 21602 1 (pb) 0 335 21603 X (hb)
ISBN-13: 978 0 335 21602 4 (pb) 978 0 335 21603 1 (hb)

Library of Congress Cataloging-in-Publication Data
CIP data applied for

Typeset by YHT Ltd, London
Printed in the UK by Bell & Bain Ltd., Glasgow
www.bell-bain.com

Contents

Acknowledgements

I want to thank those who helped make this book possible. They include those who stimulated my thinking over many years; those who supported me to write in my place of work; and those who engaged with my ideas as they changed in the process of being written.

I learnt a great deal from Michael Armstrong about the enquiring mind and the enormous intelligence of the young child. This led me to realize how much needs to be done if education is to liberate and develop that native intelligence rather than control it. Richard Winter helped me to understand the struggles and strategies involved when adults and professionals pose the difficult questions that must be asked if they are to contribute to improving the human condition. He has also been a sounding board for many of the thoughts that eventually took shape in this book's story.

I am particularly grateful to Toni Griffiths who led our attempts to create an institutional setting in which informed thoughtfulness could form the basis of development in higher education. Her comments on draft chapters were enormously helpful.

My colleagues in the Centre for the Advancement of Learning and Teaching (formerly Education and Professional Development) at University College London have been enormously supportive in giving me the space and encouragement to write. They have also lived with me through many of the struggles that come with trying to improve higher education.

I acknowledge the publishers in whose books and journals I published work which has been further developed in these pages. They are:

Chapter 2: (2003) 'Learning to comply; learning to contest', in J. Satterthwaite, E. Atkinson and K. Gale (eds) *Discourse, Power, Resistance: Challenging the Rhetoric of Contemporary Education*. Stoke-on-Trent: Trentham, pp. 13–26.

Chapter 3: (2003) 'Teaching for democracy in higher education', *Teaching in Higher Education*, 8(1): 89–101.

Chapter 5: (2002) 'Overcoming fragmentation in professional life: the challenge for academic development', *Higher Education Quarterly*, 56(1): 52–64.

Chapter 8: (2005) 'Intellectual love and the link between teaching and research', in R. Barnett (ed.) *Reshaping the University: New Relationships between Research, Scholarship and Teaching.* Milton Keynes: OUP/SRHE, pp. 92–102.

Last and most I thank Gillie Bolton who brings light and fresh air to my writing and helped me through the long dark nights of this journey.

1

Have we lost the plot or changed the story?

Loss and hope

'By going to university I hope to gain knowledge that will help me to contribute to making the world a better place.'

A group of seven academic staff from my university and a local sixth form centre were conducting some informal research into how prospective university students choose their university and subject of study. Manjit, a teacher from the centre, had asked her students to write down their immediate thoughts about this (Bhambra 2005: 8–9). Of a dozen or so scripts she presented to the group, the above comment stood out. When Manjit read it out there was a moment of surprised silence. It was the only script that expressed a purpose beyond self-interested concerns for employment, economic advantage or status. It seemed such a simple and almost obvious thing to say, yet quite out of keeping with the ways in which university entry is talked about.

Perhaps we had been reminded, by this student, of something lost: a sense of purpose that lies submerged in an educational environment that has become cynical of any idealism. I wished the student well, regardless of her, or his, A level examination results, and felt sure she or he would, indeed, make the world a better place. I hoped that the experience of studying at university would contribute to this, but was not entirely confident. After all, are universities any more directed towards improving the human condition than pharmaceutical companies, hairdressing salons or agribusinesses?

There is another sense of loss. It emerges in those all too infrequent occasions when academics meet to think together in a contemplative atmosphere. Contemplation, the exercise of curiosity, and consideration of the purposes of higher education are often seen as luxuries that can no longer be afforded in the business that now characterizes higher education. At a recent meeting with twenty academics from a Faculty of Architecture, the day was spent thinking about what it is to love one's subject and how that impacts upon how we teach and research and the relationships between them. At the end of the meeting comments were made that it was good to have intellectual conversations like this, to remind ourselves of the philosophical and political context of our work, and not to feel that we had to find immediate solutions to practical problems.

The assumption behind such comments was that university life seems no longer to contain many spaces for reflection, contemplation and open enquiry, and that the search for knowledge as an end in itself is seen to be no longer justifiable. Indeed, perhaps higher education, in the UK at least, has already internalized the view, expressed by its then Secretary of State for Education, that 'the medieval concept of scholars seeking truth ... is not (in my view) the most powerful argument for seeking state financial support' for higher education (Clarke 2003). Those who claim a central role for contemplation are often charged with social elitism (Louth 2003). Contemplation was all right for the privileged few, but not for the masses, it seems.

These opening comments on the loss of social and intellectual purposes may appear to express nostalgia. Deriving from the Greek *nostos* (return home) and *algia* (pain), this awareness of loss in higher education may be a form of homesickness: a painful memory of better times. But nostalgia inevitably involves distortion of the past, like memories of sunny childhood summers. Speaking of the conflict between the corporate ethos and the traditions of liberal higher education in the USA, Eric Gould warns us of the 'complicating politics of nostalgia inside the university' where academics 'dream of a past time when ... liberal learning was lord over all' (Gould 2003: xv–xvi). Indeed, the university never was a site for unrestrained curiosity nor for the free expression of social ideals. While we might, as academics, feel involved in a struggle – at times against the odds – to preserve intellectual and social values, there is nothing new in this. For that struggle has always been the very nature of much academic work. Indeed, as I shall argue in this book, it is the very struggle for social and intellectual values in higher education that makes it educational rather than merely the preparation of an elite for a life of privilege.

Furthermore, these two anecdotes – of the student's desire to make the world a better place and the lecturers' need for a space to think – are open to quite different interpretations. The sixth form student's idealism may remind us not so much of what has been lost, as of the irrepressible human need to serve one's fellow creatures. She feels like this despite the overbearing rhetoric of the supposed financial gains to be had from undergraduate study, delivered by ministers who, unlike her, invariably enjoyed their higher education without cost to themselves. This should give us much to hope for.

Similarly, the university staff who, given the opportunity, so readily stimulate each other's thoughts may remind us not so much of the lack of space for enquiry as of the liveliness of the academic mind. In a climate where the value of knowledge is seen almost exclusively in competitive, economic and instrumental terms, it is heartening to know that human curiosity cannot so easily be stifled.

The themes of loss and hope in relation to intellectual values will underlie much of the argument in this book. If, as I believe to be the case, higher education has indeed lost a sense of its purpose and value, the task may not be so much to attempt to regain what has been lost – the project of nostalgia – as to write a new story. This would be a story into which are woven quite fundamental social and intellectual values appropriate for a community that is concerned to understand the rapidly changing world and also to help prepare students for their place in it. The difficulty here is that the higher education community is in danger of having that story written by corporate rather than intellectual forces. Whether we are speaking of the role of research, the nature of the curriculum or other aspects of 'knowledge transfer', the problem lies in the lack of a shared story which gives an account, in the most general terms, of the purposes and practices of higher education. Such an account is required if higher education is to resist the anti-educational forces that impact upon it.

This book will attempt to outline some of the conditions that may support the university as a site for genuinely open and critical enquiry. Much has already been written about the ways in which wider social changes over the last twenty or so years have challenged, if not undermined, academic values. It has become commonplace to view the university as being in a state of crisis or in ruins (Readings 1996). We have become used to viewing learning in terms of curricula that are delivered to students who, as clients of services, pay for the added value of a higher education in order to reap economic gains. Associated with this story is that of a bureaucracy which surveys higher education and by which universities are held to account for the quality of their services. In such a climate of markets and accountability, the relationship of trust between students and their teachers is threatened.

Trust and scepticism

Onora O'Neill, in her 2002 BBC Reith Lectures (O'Neill 2002), emphasized the importance of trust to properly functioning society. She argued that a bureaucratic culture of audit – with its demands for accountability, transparency and performance indicators – can lead to its own modes of deception and thereby serve to undermine the very trust that it purports to enhance.

She notes a growth in suspicion which has led to diminishing morale amongst professionals, but at the same time comments that people continue to interact with their doctors, engineers and other public figures in a trusting manner, all the while exhibiting a culture of suspicion. Contrary to many sociologists, she concludes that in society in general there is not so much a breakdown of trust as an increase in public scepticism and suspicion.

The increase in suspicion will be familiar to many in higher education who have sought to account for themselves before the sceptical gaze of the quality assurers by producing paper trails to justify our work, or who have devised systems for closing loopholes against students who might resort to legal action in pursuit of their grievances. At the same time, in the UK, complicated games have been played by institutions and departments within them in order to ensure that the highest possible scores are achieved in research assessment exercises. As far as students are concerned, the media have become fascinated by claims that 25 per cent (Lightfoot 2004), or 54 per cent in a study at one Australian university (Szego 2003), have admitted to plagiarism. While new technologies expand the opportunities for plagiarism, similar digital technologies are developed to detect the cheats. It sometimes seems that we live in a climate in which suspicion is mutually reinforced and trust undermined by the very technology and bureaucracy that claims to enable a more open and transparent society.

The line between the lack of trust that derives from suspicion on the one hand, and healthy scepticism on the other, is a narrow one. A degree of scepticism by students towards the claims to knowledge of their teachers is a healthy sign that they want to take responsibility for their own ideas. A sceptical attitude on the part of the public towards the claims made by their political leaders is an aspect of democratic growth. A degree of scepticism towards the claims made by professionals – be they academics, lawyers, teachers or doctors – is necessary if they are to contribute to greater social justice rather than simply protect their own professional interest group. Whether such scepticism has become distorted and led to a crisis of trust may be a matter for sociological investigation. But however we make that judgement, the case I shall present is that academic enquiry must strive to build both scepticism *and* trust. Therein lies the practical wisdom whose development must be a concern for the enquiring university, or indeed for any democratic educational enterprise.

The idea of a university that consists of a community, or rather communities, of trust that celebrate informed scepticism is an ambitious one. In a climate that is characterized by complexity and fragmentation this is particularly difficult. Such a climate is inevitably one in which prediction is difficult and therefore trust is hard to maintain. But, for that very reason, an atmosphere of trust must be an important feature of university life. Enquiry – for students or researchers – involves posing difficult, risky or even dangerous questions. That demands both scepticism and trust in an environment that is complex, or indeed supercomplex.

Complexity and stability

Barnett (2000) developed an insightful conception of *supercomplexity*, which he distinguishes from *complexity*. A situation is complex, according to Barnett, when we have to choose between a range of options in the face of overwhelming data and theories, all within a frame of reference. A lecturer deciding how to organize a seminar amongst her group of students, whom she knows, might be faced with such complexity. There are competing theories about how such events might be managed and overwhelming data about the students. The situation becomes supercomplex, however, when questions are raised that go beyond this frame of reference – for example, such questions as 'Should the lecturer, rather than the students, take on this responsibility anyway?' or 'Given the pressure to achieve in the next research assessment, should I really be spending so much time trying to solve this kind of problem?' Such questions are outside the original frame of reference. According to Barnett, professional judgement is increasingly supercomplex because it is made within frames of reference that are increasingly multiplied and often in conflict. If the idea of the university is to be realized, Barnett claims, it must take account of the fact that we live in such 'an age of supercomplexity'.

The distinction is a useful one. It articulates clearly how many academics (and other professionals) feel as they struggle with the dynamics of their professional environments. The ways in which universities research, organize and teach knowledge appear to give little acknowledgement to such supercomplexity, and Barnett's ideas are much needed here. His later work (Barnett and Coate 2005) goes on to explore what a higher education curriculum might be under such conditions of uncertainty.

But is life today really more uncertain than it was in the past? It is important not to allow the politics of nostalgia to lead us to suppose that the past was more stable than the present, nor to over-dramatize our situation. It may seem to us that supercomplexity is a new phenomenon, but it may be that hindsight largely creates this illusion. Throughout history writers have spoken of chaos, disintegration and the breaking down of accepted frameworks. In the mid-nineteenth century, for example, Marx and Engels (1969), in the *Communist Manifesto*, commented that in an 'uninterrupted disturbance of all social conditions ... all that is solid melts into air' in their analysis of capitalism, which they argue to be continually expanding and revolutionizing itself to create new markets. Or sixty years later, shortly after the First World War, W. B. Yeats writes in *The Second Coming* of a new world order, as part of a cyclical process of change, in which 'Things fall apart; the centre cannot hold; mere anarchy is loosed upon the world' (Yeats [1920] 1970: ll. 3–4). Indeed, the experience of modernity has been characterized as being changeable, volatile and dynamic (Berman 1982). So perhaps supercomplexity is nothing new. And perhaps the so-called post-modern condition in general, which some claim to have superseded modernity, is also not so very different. We might view with some caution Lyotard's assertion twenty years ago that it is 'at this very Post-modern moment that finds the University nearing what may be its end' (1984: xxv). Perhaps the story of the university has not so much come to an end as to be in need of rewriting.

These are very important and difficult historical, cultural and philosophical issues which cannot be resolved in a few introductory comments. All I want to do here is to note that, in our attempts to sketch out the purposes the university might serve, we need to be wary of claims that the world today is very much more uncertain than it was in the past.

Perhaps what is important, however, is the prominence that is given to uncertainty, complexity and unpredictability in the ways our lives have come to be portrayed. Uncertainty and complexity make a good story. We are disturbed by them. They are in conflict with an increasingly technologically oriented and managed approach to life and work. The issue may not be so much the extent to which the world is unpredictable as the extent to which we are disturbed by its unpredictability. In spite of attempts to do so, the use of technology has not, in fact, made the world a more predictable or safe place. But perhaps a more technologically oriented way of thinking has made us more averse to unpredictability and its consequent risk.

This fear of unpredictability – a feature of what has come to be called the 'risk-averse society' by such commentators as Furedi (2004) – has a particular impact upon education. For if, as I shall argue in this book, there is something inevitably open and unpredictable about learning, then a risk-averse culture will be one that is inevitably hostile to learning.

Higher education curricula are increasingly conceived, and narrated, in terms of outcomes, prescriptions and predictions. Even the story of the PhD – an unpredictable journey if ever there was one – is being reconceived, by the Higher Education Funding Council for England (HEFCE), amongst others, increasingly in terms of predefined outcomes to be realized by the student in preparation for employment (Metcalfe *et al.* 2002). Where has the sense of adventure gone?

My aim for the enquiring university is to take an opposite, more adventurous, approach. I shall propose that we need to grow up and see unpredictability and risk as features of life that we should embrace in the spirit of open enquiry. I hope to show that it is in the very spaces where unpredictability, uncertainty and the need for tentativeness and provisionality are at their greatest that there are the best opportunities for building communities of enquiry.

But if the story of higher education is to be rewritten in this way – if we are to reconceive its plot in ways that emerge out of the best intellectual traditions – we need a language in which to do this. And this brings me to the final problem which I want to address in these opening comments.

A language for enquiry

In the UK, the Learning and Skills Council has played a prominent role in articulating the purposes of learning in relation to skills and employment. It is therefore perhaps ironic that, in the year in which the *Times Higher Education Supplement* awarded it for providing the best 'gobbledegook' in education (THES 2003), its chief executive commented that the 'jargon, the acronyms and the lack of clarity' needed to be replaced by a 'passionate and compelling language that reflects the excitement and challenge of the world that we work in' (Tysome 2003).

A prominent feature of this 'jargon' is the mechanical metaphor. Learning is successfully 'delivered' when teaching programmes are 'rolled out' in accordance with 'benchmarks' and have an 'impact' upon students whose performance is 'tracked' to ensure that standards are 'driven up'. Research proposals are required to state 'outputs' which fill 'gaps in knowledge' or to enhance research 'capacity'. Such a language has its roots in the factory in which inputs and outputs are controlled in order to produce quality-assured products for consumption. It portrays learning and research in ways that deny its unpredictability and its humanity. The mechanical metaphors that have come to dominate the story of higher education reflect an attempt to exercise control over an aspect of human activity that does not readily submit to control. They should have little place in an account of forms of enquiry that are essentially human.

Such mechanical metaphors and bureaucratic language are not only hostile to the traditional academic values of contemplation, open enquiry and critical study. They are also hostile to a higher education that responds to the concerns of the wider world, including employment. An employer recently interviewed in a national magazine spoke of the most important outcomes of higher education in terms of 'passion', 'integrity', 'enthusiasm' and 'openness' (Miller Smith 2002: 10). Such a view also appears to be supported by a partnership of UK, Japanese, European and Australian as well as American HE–business fora (Bok 2003; CIHE 2003), which urges universities not to relinquish scholarly values. The Director of the Council for Industry and Higher Education goes further, and suggests that universities should enable students to 'comment on and challenge political and philosophical debate on every dimension of human life' (Brown 2005: 1). Such views seem far from the narrow statements that describe policies for teaching and research. They cannot readily be expressed in terms of skills and knowledge, yet they are essential if the knowledge and skill that universities produce are to be used to the human good. If higher education is, as Manjit's sixth former put it, 'to make the world a better place', knowledge and skill must be deployed with passion, openness, humanity and the other virtues that characterize intellectual enquiry.

If bureaucratic and mechanistic language is so limited in its appropriateness for speaking about higher education, how then is higher education to tell its story? In what language is it to account for its work to the society it serves? What is the form of its narrative? And moreover, how are its practitioners – staff and students – to speak to each other in ways that acknowledge an appropriate relationship between academe and democratic society?

While university traditions which reach back over two thousand years might be helpful here, looking backwards is not enough. For the first time, universities in many countries are providing, or attempting to provide, an education for the majority of their citizens. They are aiming to open their doors to those from a wider cross-section of the community. But if higher education is genuinely to be open to a wider community, it must be open in many different ways. Indeed, openness must be a feature of the very way in which it tells its story.

An open account is one that keeps open debate, welcomes contestation and refuses to foreclose on difficulties. Unlike the language of most public relations accounts, an open language is one that is not afraid to acknowledge contradictions, does not provide immediate solutions and is prepared to upset comfortable expectations. In open forms of enquiry, rigour and precision are the result of critical questions, imaginative associations and insightful descriptions rather than narrow definitions and inappropriate quantification. A research proposal, or a curriculum document, that is open is one that recognizes the extent to which new knowledge is unpredictable. Indeed, the element of surprise in learning and research is to be welcomed rather than seen as a fortunate or unfortunate by-product or an administrative inconvenience.

An open way of speaking about higher education would also change the way 'quality' is to be understood in two important ways. First, it would distinguish quality from quantity and would therefore be wary of attempts to *reduce* assessments of quality to measures of quantity. While quantification is important, once careful analysis has revealed how it can help, the current obsession with measurement and target setting leads to systematic games playing and distortion in the service of competition.

Second, it would be much more mindful that quality is not simply the property of an object but a relation between object and subject. Thus, for example, the question of assuring quality in a university would give much more emphasis to an understanding of the purposes of the university, such as its relation to the society it serves. At present it is notable that UK universities are measured in terms that produce a plethora of league tables, but any debate concerning the relationships between such measurements of quality and purposes is almost totally absent.

Accounts of universities written in these terms would help their readers, such as prospective students, to make their own judgements from their own perspectives, without the distortion provided by numerical ranking systems. They would open up debate about higher education rather than close it off; they would engage the community and potential students and research funders in dialogue. The market place of higher education would become more a conversational forum than a competitive sales pitch. It would encourage an inclination to listen rather than proclaim.

Such open accounts would thus resist the bland descriptions of branding and managerialist language. For example, the logo of one leading UK university, proclaimed on all envelopes, is the delivery of 'excellence in teaching and research'. A language that pretends that 'the pursuit of excellence' is meaningful is, in the end, self-defeating. Such epithets are succeeded by claims to be 'world class' and then 'global', as the ways in which universities tell their stories become puffed up into increasingly cosmic proportions. A university for enquiry needs to have its feet much more firmly planted on the ground.

In their analysis of the Dearing Report (NCIHE 1997), which reported on the future of higher education in the UK, Robinson and Maskell characterized its language as being a combination of 'windy assertiveness with banality' (Maskell and Robinson 2001: 67). The situation has not improved since then. Such ways of speaking cease to be a language with which to think or listen. Its contrast with the language of the Robbins Report on Higher Education (CHE 1963), 34 years earlier, is striking. Robbins is aspirational; Dearing is instrumental. What we need is an aspirational account appropriate to the changed circumstances of the twenty-first century.

The enquiring university, then, would speak of itself in terms that are more closely rooted in the human values that it seeks to promote. Such values reflect the needs of employment in an enlightened democratic society as well as the values of intellectual enquiry. We must therefore be wary of any simplistic dichotomy between intellectual and vocational purposes.

Boundaries and context

If the enquiring university is to understand itself in more humane terms, then its work must be understood in relation to its wider context. While this is an obvious point, current discourses give this inadequate attention, particularly in the field of teaching and learning in higher education. Recent reviewers of research into learning and teaching, such as Malcolm and Zukas (2001), have analysed the ways in which learning has increasingly been discussed in terms of processes unrelated to the wider social and political context. Pedagogy has thus been discussed primarily in terms of an (often ill-understood) applied psychology unrelated to the rich literature of higher education policy. A wider conversation is needed across disciplinary boundaries and also reaching out to the wider community. Such conversation would enhance the intellectual life of the academic community and at the same time make it more accessible to the wider world.

The creation of a narrative for higher education that is enriched by the insights and methods of different disciplines presents us with perhaps the greatest challenge. For how are the critical insights from different fields to be communicated and shared across disciplinary boundaries when the language in which one discipline expresses itself is not readily understood by another? For example, the word 'critical' means one thing in a natural science and quite another in a social science; 'learning' means something very different to a psychologist and to a sociologist. Thus a university that aims to help students 'learn to be critical' might mean very different things. And if academics from different disciplines find it difficult to speak of higher education in a language that they can all understand, how can they be expected to communicate this story to a wider public that may not even share their concerns? Given this difficulty, it is perhaps unsurprising that the language in which higher education communicates with the wider world tends to be bland and shallow.

This problem is not specific only to teaching. What is meant by 'theory' is quite different in different disciplines. And when research is discussed generically, or across disciplinary boundaries, even definitions of the term 'research' are not shared by the sciences and the arts. For example, the HEFCE consultation report for its Review of Research defined scholarship as 'the reinterpretation of existing knowledge' as opposed to research, which is defined as 'new knowledge' (HEFCE 2000: 25). Now many in the arts and humanities would view criticism, interpretation and reinterpretation as being research activity, but not HEFCE, it seems. The HEFCE definition of research here would appear to reflect a set of scientific, or rather technical, presuppositions about the nature of knowledge and its discovery.

The two examples I have chosen concerning narrow understandings of learning (in psychological terms) and research (in technical terms) both privilege technical ways of thinking and speaking over more humanistic and artistic forms. This is no coincidence. For a technical language is more suited to forms of control that are the feature of bureaucratic accountability. This is not a plea to redress the disciplinary balance in higher education in favour of the arts and humanities (although such a case could well be made), but rather to indicate that higher education needs to rewrite its story in a language that is open to different disciplinary perspectives while preserving the intellectual and human aims of enquiry that are common to all. Only if this narrative can be written and understood across disciplinary boundaries will it be able to tell its story in ways that articulate with the wider human context.

Let me summarize, then, the project that I want to pursue in this book. My starting point is that higher education has lost its way. Its agendas have been driven by forces beyond its control and it has ceased to be able to provide an adequate account of its purposes. It has indeed lost the plot. To address this there is a need to acknowledge the problems and their causes in order to move beyond despair and instead be led by hope founded upon a commitment to the intellectual values that are still present within the academic community. A feature of this despair is a lack of trust within the higher education community and between it and the wider society it serves. Regaining trust is not a matter of retreating into the old cosy certainties of a more elite system, but of building upon the healthy scepticism that forms a basis of intellectual and democratic enquiry. This is difficult in a climate that is characterized by a fear of risk and unpredictability. It demands that risk be embraced as an inevitable and exciting aspect of the learning that is involved in teaching and in research.

Any attempt to achieve this will require that the story of higher education is told in a way that is not afraid to express the intellectual and human values of enquiry. Such a language would draw upon the insights of different disciplines and struggle with the problems arising from their different forms of expression. This will involve taking risks in the attempt to communicate across linguistic divides. It demands a preparedness to accept ignorance and uncertainty in the face of unfamiliar ways of thinking. Such a narrative will be more open and accessible to the wider and more divergent community with which higher education is becoming increasingly engaged.

The enquiring university is one that is able to make progress on this project, and this book aims to explore how this might be achieved.

Outline of the book

This exploration opens in the second chapter, arguing that universities have always existed in a state of tension between the demand to serve society, on the one hand, and a commitment to contesting its assumptions, perspectives and power relationships, on the other. Recent developments have shifted this balance towards a culture of compliant service to the needs of a global economy. This has highlighted the importance of teaching, but in the process has led to reductionist conceptions of quality, and undermined the role of the discipline. The emergence of more interdisciplinary forms of teaching and research may – but only under certain conditions – rekindle a more intellectual culture of contestation as academics engage in innovation and conceptual struggle around disciplinary boundaries. For this to happen universities must create and preserve the necessary intellectual spaces for enquiry amongst staff and students.

This argument is developed in more detail in Chapters 3 to 8.

Chapter 3 addresses the relationship between higher education and society, in which concerns for democratization come to the fore while the demands of an increasingly global economy have influenced educational practices towards a more utilitarian outlook. How do these changes impact upon teaching and learning and the aims they serve? The chapter will report an investigation conducted in South Africa, the UK and Russia to examine this question. While Russia and South Africa have recently undergone radical policy changes in the promotion of democracy, this has been accompanied by increased economic globalization. In the UK, on the other hand, questions of democracy have been less prominent. The study explores how university teachers in the three countries understand the relationships between their teaching and their democratic values. Their perspectives suggest that the classroom in many ways reflects, and perhaps reproduces, the values and relationships of the wider society.

One consequence of demands placed upon higher education by the global economy is the increased requirement for vocationally oriented skills training. Skills have been highlighted as an important educational outcome. At the same time, traditional approaches to university teaching have been criticized for their over-emphasis upon academic knowledge. Distinctions have been made between knowledge and skill, and categories of skills (transferable, key, employability and so on) have emerged. This presents teachers with a confusion of jargon in terms of which they are required to describe and account for their teaching. Chapter 4 will consider these issues and analyse the ways in which this can undermine the intellectual integrity of the academic subject to be taught. It is perhaps in this area, more than any other, that the need for a more coherent language for discussing the higher education curriculum is needed. An approach to overcoming these problems and developing a new language for the curriculum will be suggested.

The conflicting needs of the global economy and for democratization have acted upon higher education together with other pressures. This has led to the fragmentation of academic practice. Chapter 5 will outline the various forms this has taken. These include the lack of agreement about the purposes of higher education; the divisions between teachers and students in their relationship as provider and consumer; the remoteness of academic managers from academic practices they manage; the separation between teaching and research; and the fragmentation and commodification of knowledge itself. This chapter will discuss these aspects of fragmentation and will argue that a form of academic development is needed to attempt to reintegrate academic practice. Such a new integrity can be created in spaces where academics, with and without their students, can address matters of mutual interest. The chief of these is to (re)gain a sense of the academic purpose. This will enable the development of integrity in two senses: towards a more holistic appreciation of academic work; and towards a morally grounded practice (Macfarlane 2003).

But whose task is it to provide this academic development? Who is to initiate the enquiries that are needed to reintegrate academic life? How would such developments find a place within the current agendas for development and change? To what extent would this be a theoretical, educational or practical initiative? Chapter 6 will discuss these questions and consider the contribution that can be made to it by educationalists, educational/staff developers and academic staff from the substantive disciplines. The chapter will conclude by clarifying the need to develop the interdisciplinary field of higher educational studies whose purpose is to research, teach and raise awareness of the changing nature of academic practices so that the sector can take a more leading role in the processes of change in which it is involved.

Such a developmental project is interdisciplinary. But what is meant by interdisciplinarity? One result of the fragmentation of knowledge described in Chapter 5 has been the loss of the centrality of the discipline. But the danger for interdisciplinarity is that it lacks the critical edge of disciplinary rigour. This has been described as a feature of post-modernity, with its consequent loss of faith in the 'metanarrative' that is implied by disciplinary study (Lyotard 1984). Rather than view disciplinary perspectives as representing outmoded forms of academic culture and knowledge (as, for example, do Gibbons *et al.* 1994), Chapter 7 argues that the disciplines provide a valuable resource for critique and contestation as long as they are brought into a relationship of mutual enquiry. This concept of critical interdisciplinarity will be developed as constituting a form of enquiry in which different frameworks of assumptions and theories are brought into critical engagement. This will be distinguished from the forms of multi-disciplinary practice in which knowledge from the constituent disciplinary fields can be viewed as commodities which can be added together. The chapter will go on to examine the various ways in which critical inter-disciplinarity is blocked by institutional and conceptual difficulties and the ways in which these blocks might be addressed.

Much of the discussion so far has argued for the need for bringing teachers, researchers and students together in conversations across disciplines and the other divides in the professional field. But what is the nature of enquiry that characterizes such conversations? And what is the place of enquiry in relation to teaching and research?

In Chapter 8, with reference to a range of thinkers since Plato who have argued for open forms of enquiry, I develop the concept of 'intellectual love' as articulated by the rationalist seventeenth-century philosopher Spinoza. This provides an appropriate basis for understanding academic enquiry. It indicates an approach that brings teaching and research into a closer relationship. It also provides a framework for reinterpreting some of the recent research into the links between teaching and research and indicates the need to build cultures of enquiry, appropriate to the present day, in order to enhance these links and bring a new intellectual integrity to university work.

In the final chapter I draw together the ideas of the earlier chapters, and subject them to critique, by using them to address quite specific practical problems that academic staff face in their daily work as they attempt to manage the competing demands placed upon their time. It will consider the possibilities for real change that can emerge from practice on a small scale and suggest ways in which appropriate critical responses can be made to bureaucratic and managerialist demands. The chapter will lead towards a perspective of hope and realization that we may not be quite as powerless as we sometimes feel.

2

Compliance and contestation

The intellectual should constantly disturb, should bear witness to the
misery of the world, should be provocative by being independent,
should rebel against all hidden and open pressure and manipulations,
should be the chief doubter of systems, of power and its incantations,
should be a witness to their mendacity.

(Havel 1990: 167)

The skills, creativity and research developed through higher education
are a major factor in our success in creating jobs and in our prosperity.

(DfES 2003: 4)

Introduction

Higher education and its staff are cajoled, criticized and pressurized to
change, innovate and adapt. The celebration of intellectual values plays
little part in academic life. Indeed, the very idea of 'intellectual values' is
one that is viewed with suspicion as relating to a monastic past rather than
the needs of society at large. Compliance, rather than the rational debate,
has become the predominant feature of the way higher education manages
its affairs.

At the same time, the way universities organize knowledge, which is their
basic product, is changing. Increasingly freed from traditional academic
constraints, the whole idea of categorizing knowledge into 'disciplines' is
being challenged. This can lead to exciting opportunities. But there is also a
deeply disturbing trend which needs to be understood and resisted if it is
not to undermine the whole enterprise.

There never has been, nor could there ever be, a Golden Age in which
the pursuit of educational ideals is an easy ride. As Confucius put it: 'No
vexation, no enlightenment; no anxiety, no illumination' (Huang 1997:
163). The discovery of new knowledge or trying to understand what is

known is, to some extent, a vexatious and anxious business. It is inevitably a struggle to create, maintain and enhance the climate for learning. That struggle is a fundamental part of learning itself, not merely an unfortunate condition to be resolved before learning can take place.

Furthermore, if higher education is directed towards creating a more democratic society, the struggle is twofold. Democracy, like learning, inevitably involves anxiety, courage and discomfort in the face of forces that oppose it. Contestation is thus a feature of the struggle for learning and for democracy.

The relationship between compliance and contestation has much to do with how we understand learning: what kind of thing it is, how it happens and what its purposes might be. In discussing these matters my focus will be on the learning of students, lecturers, research workers and others who support the enterprise: indeed the whole 'learning community' (Schuller 1995: 44–50). I shall often use the term 'enquiry' – a concept that will be explored more fully in Chapter 8 – to indicate learning in these contexts of teaching, research and support.

Education as a critical service

In the days when the Church was the most powerful social institution, universities served its needs by preserving the doctrine and training clerics. Later, throughout the period of imperial expansion, universities took on a major function of training the elite – the administrators and the leading professionals – and providing much of the scientific knowledge that underpinned the industrial revolution. There have been further shifts in political power and the relationship between universities and society. Now we are moving into a period where, according to commentators such as Klein (2001) and Hertz (2001), the major source of power in our post-industrial society is no longer the Church or even the state but the global economy. The global knowledge-based economy now shapes higher education. The *New Rulers of the World* (Pilger 2002) are the globally oriented transnational corporations or, if one accepts Pilger's analysis, the single superpower whose military capability supports their interests. Universities now serve these economic interests. National governments are becoming the means by which these global interests are served.

This shift of power towards global corporations has been associated with greatly increased inequality. At the start of the twenty-first century, the combined assets of the world's 225 richest people were roughly equal to the annual incomes of the poorest 47 per cent (Heintz and Folbre 2000); and the total value of eight companies was greater than the combined wealth of half the world's population (World Development Movement 2001). It is within such an unequal society that higher education contributes its service. In this context, we can expect higher education institutions to become increasingly for-profit organizations, following the lead that the USA is making in this market (THES 2004). The World Trade Organization is actively promoting this movement through its General Agreement on Trade in Services (GATS) in which, under US pressure, higher education is becoming conceived as a service to be opened up to the market. In the UK, the Association of University Teachers views this development as part of the 'McDonald's-ization' (*sic*) of higher education (AUT 2003: 6).

While the distribution of power in society has changed, the relationship of service between the university and society has not. As before, social, economic and political forces ensure that universities (like other institutions) serve the needs of society. As before, we live in a society in which power and influence are far from equal. Universities are therefore inevitably under pressure from the powerful forces within society – be they the Church, the nation state, or the global economy.

This simple analysis, however, is in tension with an opposing way of looking at the role of the university. The roots of this opposing view can be traced back through John Dewey (1939) to the Enlightenment of the eighteenth century, or even further back to the Greek traditions of scholarship developed by Plato and Aristotle. It is a view that is at odds with the narrow economistic view above but is not necessarily at odds with the views of employers who are seeking to attract graduate employees. The interests of the majority of employers and future employees who are subject to the market are not the same as those of multinational corporations which exert power over the market. Neither are they the same as those of government which often claims to represent their interests.

According to this opposing view, the role of the academy has always been to critique existing knowledge, and contest the assumptions and the social forces that shape people's ways of thinking. It is through reason, careful observation and critical analysis that universities contribute to freeing society from the forces of unreason and prejudice. The role of the university, from this point of view, is not to serve the needs of the powerful but to liberate us through the power of critical reasoning. The university, through scholarship, enables us not so much to serve and comply with the world as we find it, but to contest what we find and imagine how it might be different. From this perspective, reasoned deliberation is the means by which the university enhances society's capacity to reflect and promote the values of democracy and social justice.

This discussion could be continued. For example, it might be observed that those who have been fortunate enough to enter higher education in order to engage in such critical scholarship have only ever been the relatively privileged in the first place. One cannot therefore consider how access to higher education is to be widened without also considering the unequal distribution of power in society which perpetuates such privilege. Government advisers such as Adonis (1998) in the UK and Reich (2004) in the USA have acknowledged this. Less readily considered, however, is the implication that the very concepts of academic excellence and the maintenance of standards can only be understood in relation to a social and political context in which the distribution of wealth, power and privilege is unequal.

There are thus two analyses. According to one, the university serves society by preparing people for work. According to the other, the university is society's scholarly critic in the furtherance of democracy. These two analyses exist in tension and are, in fact, both present at any time. This idea is not new. It was nicely expressed in the context of schooling in the USA by Carnoy and Levin (1985: 4): 'The relationship between education and work is dialectical – composed of a perpetual tension between the two dynamics, the imperatives of capital and those of democracy in all its forms.'

I now want to take this idea further, however, and suggest that a similar dialectic operates in relation to learning. For universities to work within such tensions requires imagination. As the mathematician and philosopher A.N. Whitehead (1929: 145) put it: 'The proper function of a university is the imaginative acquisition of knowledge … A university is imaginative or it is nothing – at least nothing useful.'

Learning to comply or learning to contest

The individual learner's relationship with the teacher, as well as the university's relationship with the wider society, can be viewed as a dynamic tension between compliance and contestation. To explore this, consider what is taking place right here and now as I write this book and you, my reader, read it.

Reading and writing are instances of learning and teaching. They typify what takes place in educational institutions: students learn from, amongst other things, texts that teach them. You are probably not an undergraduate student, but you are performing as a learner and I, in my authorial role, am performing as the teacher. I am attempting to engage you in a subject matter of my choosing by sharing some of my understanding, and hoping that you will gain something of value from the reading.

Now as I write this, I wonder what my reader might learn from it. But since this form of communication (like the formal lecture) precludes any kind of conversation at this point, I'm not able to check up on how it is going to be received. If I am successful you may avoid falling asleep and continue to the end of the chapter, at least. You may feel that you have some grasp of what I am trying to say and may remember afterwards the gist of the chapter. If I do a really good job, I may altogether engage you and you may feel you have a clear idea of what I wanted to communicate and may want to continue to the end of the book. In that case, you will have complied with my expectations about what I had to write (or teach), and both my performance as a writer (teacher) and yours as a reader (learner) will have conformed to the best predictions regarding its outcome. In principle, each chapter in this book could, in traditional old-fashioned textbook style, be followed by a test to check up that all had gone according to plan.

Such an account of reading and writing has been likened to the passing of a message from the full vessel of the author/teacher to the empty vessel of the reader/student (Readings 1996: 150–65). I have described this as the 'didactic model' of teaching and learning (or writing and reading) (Rowland 1993: 19–22). Others have used Freire's metaphor of 'banking' and building 'capital' to describe what the learner does with the resulting knowledge (1972: 45). It has become fashionable to reject such 'passive' accounts of learning. That is not my purpose here. Rather I shall contrast it with another perspective.

Another view of the nature of writing and reading – or teaching and learning – takes into account the contribution made by the reader. For example, what I have written here may shed light upon the reader's experience or it may directly conflict with it. It may, or may not, be imbued with values that the reader shares. Its argument might seem insightful, but it may appear to be flawed by an illogical sequence of ideas. It may appear to be skilfully written or to be a misuse of language. You may, after reading the book, reflect further on some of the things I have written. You may even want to reconsider your past experience and come to see it a little differently in the light of your reading, or you may compare my ideas with others you have heard or read about or with the ideas of friends. With all this going on, your interpretation or reading of what I have to say will be different from the next person's and from mine.

Now this second account gives life to the reader (learner) as an active participant. Such active reading radically changes the relationship between writer and reader, or teacher and learner. This 'birth of the reader', as Barthes puts it, 'must be at the cost of the death of the author' (1977: 143–8). This might seem a somewhat dramatic way of envisaging my future as author of this text, but it highlights the way in which readers (or the audience of a lecture or the member of a facilitated group discussion) create their own meanings. Texts or lessons, lectures or workshops, are constructed, or reconstructed, by the reader who does not have access to the author's intentions, even with the most detailed statements of 'intended outcomes' in course documentation. Even where such statements are made explicit they are, like any other texts, open to interpretation and reinterpretation.

The distinction I am making here goes beyond the distinction often made between so-called 'active' and 'passive' learning. It also highlights the very limited extent to which any author, or teacher, can predict or control the outcomes for the reader or learner.

Such an approach to reading this book presupposes an engagement that is active, critical, reflective and imaginative. The author's contribution is acknowledged to be open to question, contestable, and open to different interpretations. For that reason, no simple end-of-chapter test is likely to shed much light on the complexity of the reader's thoughts, reflections, feelings and imaginings. To make matters worse – worse, that is, as far as our ability to assess this educational experience goes – it may be that some of your reflections are further reflected upon at some point in the future. Perhaps there emerges a train of thinking, which continues long after you have forgotten all about reading this. But you won't know about that until it happens, and may even then be unaware of the links.

In my first account of reading this chapter, the assumption was that ideally the reading should conform to the author's intentions. In the second account, the reading is assumed to be critical, contestable and imaginative. This argument, however, can be extended to apply to any form of learning interaction. Lectures, group discussions, computer-mediated communications, and so on, can all be viewed as texts which are intended to lead to certain prescribed outcomes. Alternatively, they can be viewed as texts that learners construct and reconstruct in the light of their critical readings.

There are thus two ways of thinking about learning and the teacher, just as there are two ways of thinking about the university and society: the first account privileges compliance, predictability and control; the second, contestation, novelty and freedom. The point of making this distinction is not to argue that contestation, rather than compliance, should underpin our thinking about universities and teaching. Rather we have to acknowledge that the university, and the approach to its practices of teaching and research, functions within an inevitable tension between the proper demand to comply and to serve, and also to be critical. Enquiry works within that tension as a *critical service*.

It has been suggested that this idea of critical service is an ancient one, and draws upon the writings of the Greek philosopher and rhetor Isocrates (436–338 BC), who was concerned to reunite the individual with the social, theory with practice and critique with service within the city state of Ancient Greece (Clark 1996). The ways in which enquiry can work within this dynamic will be developed further in Chapter 8.

Recent developments in the light of this dynamic

The dominant public discourse on learning can be viewed in relation to this dynamic of compliance and contestation. What emerges appears to be a conception of higher education in which compliance becomes an imperative that risks undermining the university's critical foundations (Coffield 1999).

For example, in the UK a Minister of State for Higher Education said at a public lecture that the major function of the university, as far as teaching was concerned, was to meet the skill shortage in the global market place (Blackstone 2001). Such a view was not contestable, was stated as a matter of fact, and was presumed to be common sense. It clearly portrayed the university as providing a compliant service to the market. She was not suggesting that the imperatives of the market place might be questioned by scholarly investigation; not envisaging that the university might question the relationships of power between the rich and poor within which the markets operate; she was not suggesting that the university might be concerned about the interests served by the global market place and how they might impact upon social justice. She took it for granted that the market will and should be in control, and that the universities will comply by providing the services demanded of them. Many commentators, such as Friedman (2000), support this view of globalization as being an irresistible and transformative power, transforming education just as it transforms other social institutions and practices.

This one-way transaction between education and society mirrors a one-way transaction between teacher and learner. For here we find that a similar relationship of compliance and conformity is assumed to be desirable. The subsequent UK Minister of State for Higher Education, speaking about her time as a university student some thirty years earlier, said in her first interview with the press that she recollected that she had done very little work (Hodge 2001). She only got a third class degree. 'I should have been forced to do more work,' she said, 'it was outrageous.'

Now no doubt she should have done more work, but she is here holding her teachers, rather than herself, responsible for her shortcomings. Again we can see the implication that the teacher should force compliance upon the student, whose response should be one of servility and conformity to expectations. In her view, responsibility for learning (or lack of it, in her case) lies with the teacher, not the learner.

These two examples serve to illustrate the emphasis that is currently placed upon a compliant relationship between higher education and society, and between students and their teachers.

At the same time, various central initiatives in the UK and elsewhere have encouraged academics to think more seriously about how students evaluate the teaching they receive. Money has been made available to encourage the development of innovative approaches to teaching, and to explore the potential of new technologies. Programmes of work for students offer them a greater choice of subjects. Additional forms of support for students have been developed in order to improve their ability to study. They have been encouraged to develop skills, rather than academic knowledge on its own. Students have been encouraged to become more active learners, to reflect upon their own learning, and take responsibility for it, rather than merely to respond passively. Indeed, there has been a shift from an emphasis upon teaching towards an emphasis on learning. With their differences in interests, abilities and backgrounds, students have been put at the centre stage of teaching and learning.

Such changes would appear to acknowledge the more imaginative aspects of learning and to support critical scholarship, rather than conformity and compliance, amongst students.

When one takes into account the wider political context, however, a rather different picture emerges. In the UK, the funds spent on educating each university student fell 36 per cent between 1989 and 1997 (DfES 2003), with a further small fall since then. While this decrease in funding per student can be understood as the result of rapidly increasing numbers of students, the expansion of higher education has still not shifted the predominantly middle-class population that university serves. In 2002, young people from professional backgrounds were still five times as likely to get into higher education as people from non-professional backgrounds (DfES 2003).

As a consequence of this expansion in numbers without commensurate expansion of funding, measures have been devised for ensuring (or assuring) that teaching and learning are effective and that the reduced resources from the public purse are well spent. Consequently, a bureaucratic account of learning has emerged in order to quantify and compare the performance of institutions by making supposedly objective assessments of effectiveness.

My first account of reading this chapter, in which I suggested that the reader might learn what I intended, was easy to assess. The second, in which I speculated about the variety of ways in which the reader might respond, was difficult to assess with any accuracy. The need to provide objective, numerical assessments of the effectiveness of teaching or learning inevitably prioritizes the former way of looking at learning as a predictable and limited activity. Under this regime, teaching is presumed to consist in the delivery of a text whose meaning is presumed to be transparent.

Understandably, if we want to ensure value for money, we need to be able to predict and measure. The fact that learning – or at least the more imaginative or critical aspects of learning – does not so readily submit to prediction and measurement is indeed unfortunate.

This prioritization of conformity and predictability impacts upon how courses are planned, upon the way students are taught, and upon the way learning and teaching are evaluated. For example, when academic staff design curricula, the templates they are required to follow and questions they have to answer presuppose a particular view of the curriculum. This is a view that the curriculum to be learnt necessarily has definable outcomes, that these outcomes can be measured, and thus the effectiveness of provision assessed. Lecturers have to assume that they should be able to give a measurable, or at least observable, account of the outcomes for the student. While this might be possible as far as the author's or the teacher's intentions are concerned, such intentions take little account of the unpredictable, long-term and individual response of the reader or learner.

Scholarly work has been described as the struggle 'to produce out of the chaos of the human experience some grain of order won by the intellect' (Annan 1999: 53). Such intelligence and intellectual struggle cannot be reduced to predictable outcomes, however politically and administratively convenient this might be. Much research through the 1960s, 1970s and 1980s in the schools sector demonstrated that a curriculum is a much more complex and unpredictable affair, much more like my second account of this chapter: more dependent upon what the learner contributes to the process. Such a view of the curriculum was perhaps best articulated by Stenhouse (1975) as a basis for curriculum research and development. Academic research and student learning are both forms of enquiry, and an essential feature of any enquiry is that one does not know the outcome before it starts.

So whilst many of these recent developments have been designed to shed more light on students' learning and recognize its diverse and creative nature, a regime of audit and accountability has emerged which is seriously undermining this intended effect by emphasizing compliance and pre-dictability at the expense of critique and imagination. The dynamic between the two is lost and replaced by a form of reductionism which trivializes the richness of human experience.

The changing disciplines

So far I have presented a somewhat gloomy picture of compliance. I now want to look more optimistically at the disciplines and interdisciplinary work and how recent developments here might support a more lively culture in which contestation plays its proper part.

It has been claimed that academics often join their profession because of their love of teaching (Boyer 1990). Many studies, however, particularly from the kinds of institutions described as 'research-led', suggest that most identify themselves primarily in terms of their discipline (Squires 1987; Rowland *et al.* 1998). Academics tend to see themselves as historians or engineers who teach, and indeed often enjoy teaching, rather than primarily as teachers who have history or engineering as their subject.

A discipline is not simply a body of knowledge but a way of coming to know. Noel Annan, the Vice Chancellor of the University of London (1978–81) described the importance of students coming to understand the struggle involved:

> Universities exist to cultivate the intellect. Everything else is secondary
> ... A university is dead if the dons cannot in some way communicate to
> the students the struggle – and the disappointments as well as the
> triumphs of that struggle – to produce out of the chaos of human
> experience some grain of order won by the intellect.
>
> Annan (1999: 26)

Disciplines shape the kind of order students and researchers create and the ways they carry out the struggle.

Different disciplines involve different priorities about their purposes, different kinds of questions and different ways of answering them. An engineer, an architect and an ecologist might have very different ideas about what constitutes a good bridge, or an appropriate bridge in a particular situation. Thus we might say that from an engineering point of view, or from an ecological point of view, this or that is a preferable design. Similarly, a sociologist and a historian are likely to have different ideas about the significance of a painting, and different again from the viewpoint of an art critic whose speciality is painting.

During the last thirty years or so the disciplines have undergone radical changes as a result of two developments.

First, there has been a rapid increase in the rate at which knowledge – or at least accounts of knowledge – has increased. During the 1990s the worldwide literature in the field of chemistry, for example, grew by more than half a million articles per year. At that rate, four full-time research assistants would be needed merely to read the *titles* of chemistry articles as they are produced. In the sciences, 8500 different specialities were recently identified (Clark 2000).

Second, research and teaching have been more geared towards serving the economy. Now such practical or commercial needs invariably require knowledge from different disciplines. Providing water in an undeveloped region, for example, requires sociological and ecological knowledge and probably political and botanical knowledge, as well as engineering.

This rapid expansion of knowledge, together with the emphasis upon the profitable purposes to which it might be put, has led to the emergence of new disciplines, new combinations of discipline, challenges to existing disciplinary boundaries and the emergence of a field of studies devoted to the study of disciplinarity (Messer-Davidow 1993). It has impacted directly upon research and upon the courses we offer students.

One result of this has been curriculum modularization: courses of study have in many places been split into fragments or modules, enabling hybrid courses to be constructed by students selecting different modules from different disciplines or fields of study. Now while it has been argued that this gives students greater freedom of choice and enables courses to be constructed flexibly to suit the needs of the market, such freedom comes at a cost. The cost is often the lack of coherence of courses of study, with consequent shallowness of learning and inadequate opportunity for students to get to grips with any particular discipline (Winter 1996).

It is now more widely recognized that modularization has been driven by concerns for efficiency and administrative convenience rather than an educational conception of student-centred learning. For in such a context learners are treated as consumers in a supermarket, picking and mixing educational commodities with little sense of continuation and development. Often called 'multidisciplinary', such courses can, in fact, become non-disciplinary since the depth of study is insufficient to enable learners to engage with the critical approaches, values and paradigms of any particular discipline. A Dean of an American college, addressing staff who teach on multidisciplinary liberal arts courses, spoke of how the result can be that 'they fall into an eclecticism that does little work on any discipline; it is more entropic than transgressive' (Struppa 2002). Entropy – an increase in disorderliness – results from the lack of real disciplinary engagement. Transgression, on the other hand, is involved in moving out of the familiar territory of one discipline that has been mastered, into that of another where the same rules do not hold. Interdisciplinary work that is critical and involves contestation is inevitably transgressive.

While a broad range of studies can provide for a valuable tertiary education, the greatest value of working across different disciplines is only achieved when learners (as students or researchers) begin to grapple with the contesting and often conflicting values, purposes and approaches that underlie different disciplines. This is a process of critical reflection upon knowledge. Such critical reflection should be at the heart of what is meant by a higher education.

Interdisciplinarity and contestation

Disciplines thrive on informed contestation. Einstein's work on the development of physics, for example, challenged taken-for-granted mathematical models used to investigate the physical world. This influenced philosophical perspectives about the nature of reality. His ideas about the relativity of space–time, although rooted in the physical sciences, contributed to more relativistic ways of thinking in the humanities and social sciences. The appropriateness of this transfer of ideas from one field into another has been widely contested. There is no doubt, however, that they offered a challenge to accepted ways of thinking in other disciplines.

Challenges to disciplines often emerge when metaphors and images that underpin them are adopted by other disciplines. Chaos theory (Prigogine and Stengers 1985; Gleick 1988), for example, arose from research initially conducted in order to try to predict the ways in which the flow of fluids varies with temperature, an important matter for meteorologists. This theoretical perspective led to very general ideas about the relationships between states of chaos and states of order. Some of the scientists who worked in the field later employed their ideas and theories in an attempt to understand how predictions might be made concerning the sometimes orderly, and sometimes chaotic, behaviour of share prices and stock markets.

Later, ideas from chaos theory were taken up in the field of education (Green and Bigum 1990) and in management and economics – with titles such as *Chaos, Management and Economics* (Parker and Stacey 1994). The notion of chaos has now become the jargon of a clique of management gurus. The ways in which evidence is used and inferences made in the more sober field of criminal law, have also been subjected to analyses based upon chaos theory and its associated mathematical concept of non-linearity (Schum 2003). Even the unpredictable workings of Osama Bin Laden and al-Qaida are claimed by some to be analysable in terms of such ideas (Meek 2001).

Theories derived from one context of knowledge cannot, however, simply be transferred into another. Claims have been made that the many applications of theory from one discipline into another – particularly amongst post-modern philosophers – have amounted to an intellectual imposture (Sokal and Bricmont 1998) that aims to aggrandize academics while hiding their sloppy thinking. Such claims will be considered in more detail in Chapter 7. Here I merely want to assert that under certain conditions, when fired by curiosity that is rigorously disciplined, such applications and translations can be imaginative, playful and insightful.

Children are, of course, specialists when it comes to the playful transfer of ideas across fields of experience. Studies of the primary school classroom (Armstrong 1980; Rowland 1984) illuminate the delighted intelligence of young children discovering, for example, how such dry things as multiplication tables can be represented by satisfying patterns, and later, that interesting shapes and patterns can be understood in terms of numbers. Experienced as play, such activity can give new meaning to how children understand numbers and design, and the relationship between these two initially different areas of their experience. Such creative leaps of imagination are as important, though perhaps much more difficult, in the learning of the university researcher as they are in the learning of the young child.

Interdisciplinary learning and research also offer the possibility of contesting conceptions of identity and professional role. For example, in the UK, stimulated by the interests of the previous Chief Medical Officer (Calman 2000: xiv), and drawing upon experience in the USA, there has been a recent development of a field called medical humanities. One might suppose medicine to involve humanistic as well as scientific understanding, since it involves the application of science to the human condition. Recently, however, the President of the General Medical Council in the UK accused his own profession of expressing a culture based upon a narrowly scientific outlook towards patient care (Irvine 2001). The field of medical humanities can be seen as an attempt to correct such a narrowly scientific bias.

The exciting interdisciplinary possibility here is that insights from the humanities will contest accepted norms in medical practice, while the demands of medical practice will produce new insights in these humanities. In the process, the very idea of what it is to be a doctor on the one hand, or an artist or poet on the other, will be informed by such an engagement between humanistic and scientific forms of enquiry.

Such a development involves argument and contestation as the presumptions and practices in the different fields confront each other. Such contestation would contribute to the development of the disciplines of medicine and the humanities.

Some implications

In order for this interdisciplinary approach to fulfil its potential, with the consequent intellectual challenges for students and academic staff, opportunities need to be provided for students and staff to meet and engage with each other across disciplinary boundaries. Spaces have to be created where uncomfortable questions can be asked and tentative ideas explored without the continual fear of failure that too often dominates academic life.

This needs to be a real engagement with the intellectual work of teaching and research. It is not sufficient for staff to meet merely in order to manage procedures, or students to engage with one area of study after another without exploring the conflicts and differences between them.

It also means that teaching and learning, like research, must be focused on and motivated by a passion for the subject. Without this, contestation is trivial. In the current climate of accountability and risk aversion, terms like 'passion' and 'love of the subject' never figure in the prescriptions and requirements of central agencies with their focus upon developing skills, gaining qualifications and maintaining standards.

Interdisciplinary work offers the potential for contestation to play a more prominent part in the learning that is involved in both teaching and research. It can provide an antidote to the culture of compliance that currently predominates. It requires, however, that we have the confidence to step outside our disciplinary boundaries, not leaving that disciplinary identity behind, but being prepared to engage in a scholarly way with colleagues and students (and indeed the wider public) who may not share our priorities, assumptions or specialised languages. To put it another way, academic 'tribalism' (Becher 1989) must become more multicultural, or rather intercultural.

Interdisciplinary engagement of this sort, with its conflicting values and priorities, can feel unpredictable as the existing assumptions of one discipline are challenged by those of another. This unpredictability – like the unpredictability of what the reader might learn from the author's text – is an essential feature of enquiry, research and education. In a society that has become increasingly unpredictable it is important that those who teach, as well as their students, acknowledge their inability to predict the outcome of the search for knowledge, rather than pretend that learning can be reduced to the predictable.

Higher education is moving into a new set of relationships with the wider social and economic world. Exciting possibilities are emerging, and attention is increasingly being focused upon the contribution that learning and research can make to the wider community. Ways must be found, however, to create and protect the space to stimulate debate, contestation and imagination amongst students, staff and the wider community. These are as necessary conditions of higher education as they are of democracy itself. The struggle to create these kinds of spaces may take the form of resistance in the face of the forces of compliance. That is indeed, as Confucius put it, a 'vexatious and anxious task'.

Conclusions

In this chapter I have sketched out how higher education is inevitably a site of conflicting pressures. On the one hand, it has to work within the constraints imposed by the society it serves and the established disciplines of knowledge that it develops. On the other, it seeks to challenge those constraints in order to work towards a more democratic society and new forms of knowledge. This tension between compliance and contestation cannot simply be resolved: it is in the nature of higher education to work within this conflictual space.

At present, however, the demands to comply have the upper hand over the need to contest. While the university should be viewed as a critical servant of the wider society, at present it portrays itself as a rather compliant one. The despair that many who work in universities feel is a consequence of the lack of opportunity for genuinely critical enquiry. Critical enquiry plays little part in the language in which the story of higher education is told.

Some new ways of thinking about learning, teaching and research offer the possibility and the hope of reconstructing the critical purpose of the university as a place for intellectual enquiry. To realize these possibilities it will be necessary to create the spaces in which staff and students can take risks and can struggle to overcome the difficulties of engaging with ideas that are often framed in very different disciplinary languages.

This sketch, however, raises many themes and unanswered questions which need to be addressed. For example, where are we to find such spaces in a higher education community that appears to be increasingly fragmented? Whose job is it to create them and what kind of work is this? And if forms of interdisciplinary engagement have the potential to be fruitful, how can this potential be realized so as to enable critical interdisciplinarity and transgression, rather than the entropy of shallow eclecticism?

In discussing many of these themes I use the term 'enquiry' to indicate learning that may be independent, may be a consequence of teaching, or may be the result of research. But more precision is needed than this. Many who work in higher education experience the demands of teaching and of research to pull in quite opposite directions, yet the very term 'university' is often taken to indicate that research and teaching are complementary activities. A conception of 'enquiry' is needed that helps overcome the very real difficulties of establishing an appropriate relationship between them. So what exactly is meant by 'enquiry' and how can this bring teaching and research into a more productive relationship?

These questions will be addressed in the ensuing chapters. But first I want to consider in more detail how the different purposes of the university impact directly upon the actual business of teaching and thinking about learning. For example, how does a concern for a critical and democratic perspective that promotes social justice relate to methods of teaching? On the other hand, how does the demand that higher education provide a skilled workforce for the global economy impact upon the way we conceive of learning?

Behind these questions is an awareness that the practices of learning in higher education cannot be separated from considerations of their purposes. Current ways of thinking about learning in higher education often appear to address questions of how people learn as if learning were a technique, method or even skill which can be applied to different situations irrespective of its wider purposes and context. For example, the influential Dearing Report (NCIHE 1997) emphasized that an important function of higher education in the development of lifelong learning was to develop the student's ability to 'learn how to learn'. While the experience of learning in one domain no doubt leads to the individual being better able to learn in some other domains, its effectiveness and its methods are highly dependent upon the wider purposes to which it is put. Learning directed towards competitive self-advancement, for example, is very different from learning aimed at creating a more equal society. In this obvious sense learning is political and the ways in which we learn, and its effectiveness, relate to the social or political ends that it serves.

These are the themes that I shall take up in the next chapter. If the ways in which teaching and learning are practised are, as I am suggesting, related to their wider purposes, how does this relationship manifest itself? Does the teacher's understanding of the democratic aims of higher education impact upon the methods of teaching? To what extent is teaching a political activity?

3

Teaching for democracy

Introduction

'Freedom is not free ... democracy is not free. If you want democracy you have to fight for it. Not fight, perhaps, but *do something* about it.' This was a lecturer in sociology from a prominent Russian university telling me about his teaching in the context of recent changes in his country. Like the prospective university student who opened the first chapter saying that she wanted to make the world a better place, he understands higher education to be a moral project.

In the last chapter I argued that if higher education is to be directed towards creating a more democratic society, this will involve contestation and critique. But how might a desire to promote democracy shape the ways lecturers teach, what they teach and the ways they relate to their students? Do they even *think* about their teaching in terms of democratic considerations, and should they? I have also claimed that teaching and learning should be understood in the wider social and political context. But how does this wider context affect the way university teachers think about democracy and its relationships to their teaching?

These are the questions I shall now explore by drawing upon research I conducted in Russia, South Africa and the United Kingdom. I elicited the views of colleagues from these three countries because the national policy of each explicitly identifies the purposes of higher education in terms of democratic aims. The National Educational Policy Act of South Africa states that educational policy should contribute to 'the advancement of democracy' (South Africa 1996); the Russian 1992 Law on Education was built upon changes over the previous decade under the slogan 'more democracy' (OECD 1998: 65); in the UK the Dearing report specifically identified the development of democracy as being one of the main purposes of higher education (NCIHE 1997).

The place of democracy in the history and development of each country, however, is very different. The meanings given to the term and its connotations are fluid. The struggle for democracy may be a radical movement against a totalitarian regime. In a different context, however, the spreading of 'freedom and democracy' may provide a justification for American military intervention in the Middle East. Or democracy may be seen, linking diversity with inclusivity, as a fundamental precondition of the free market.

Might such differences be reflected in lecturers' approaches to teaching? Do national policies about the democratic purposes of higher education in fact have any impact upon the ways lecturers teach? Is a concern for democracy in society reflected in a democratization of the classroom?

Having been involved over several years in academic links and development programmes with South African, Russian and British universities, I was ideally placed to interview lecturers from these countries about teaching and democracy. I wrote to about ten from each country asking them if they would be prepared to be interviewed. They represented a cross-section of disciplines and, in South Africa, the cross-section of ethnic groups.

They all, however, professed a particular interest in teaching. Furthermore, the initial letter inviting them to take part also described the research in terms of the links with democracy. For these reasons the interviewees were not, and were not intended to be, representative of the views of lecturers in general, or of those from their country. The purpose of reporting the study here is rather to begin to explore the different ways in which teaching can promote, or respond to, democratic considerations and how these considerations might vary in the different national contexts.

My contacts all agreed to take part in hour-long open-ended conversations in which I was anxious not to imply any particular significance to the term 'democracy'. Rather than subject their ideas to any great depth of analysis, or superimpose an artificial coherence on their stories, I shall attempt to represent them naturalistically around the themes that emerged.

Teaching methods and democracy

Many of my respondents spoke of a direct relationship between democratic considerations in their teaching and in society at large. However, 'active methods of teaching [learning?] are not always directly connected to a sense of democracy', as one South African lecturer put it. Any discussion of methods must be seen in the context of the purposes it serves and the values it expresses. Notwithstanding this, his criticism of lectures extended beyond simply their ineffectiveness, to considering how lectures symbolized anti-democratic relationships. The (typically) white academic lecturing the black student masses can easily be seen to represent the relationships of a past apartheid era. Another (non-African) lecturer of largely African students described how his more interactive method of teaching served democratic purposes:

(It) is really helping in trying to actually make the Africans sometimes feel that we are all in one battle and it is not us against them, because if you look at the traditional sort of teaching what it does is basically isolate the person in front. You are never part of the masses and you are never seen to be there, and it could perpetuate the sort of separation that we already have.

Some said how it was difficult, if not impossible, to reflect their educational values through the lecture format. A Russian lecturer who acknowledged the importance of democratic considerations expressed what several appeared to have in mind in describing how the lecture communicates the wrong expectations about teaching:

> Often a teacher can achieve perfection because he is sure in his professional knowledge as a teacher ... they think they are perfect actors on a stage, and the students love these teachers and they listen to them with wide open mouths because it is a performance ... but I don't think this is a real teacher ... the aim of the teacher is not just to show off.

Such a view warns us against placing too much significance upon the satisfaction rating that students often give as a measure of teaching quality. As Johnson (2000) demonstrates, a dependence upon measures of student satisfaction does not necessarily serve educational (let alone democratic) interests.

Many of the lecturers from all three countries remarked on how their own teaching had moved away from lecturing, although this was not always easy to achieve.

The term 'responsibility' was used more than any other to describe what lecturers were trying to encourage in moving away from the lecturing format. Several explicitly identified responsibility as a condition of democratic citizenship. The development of responsibility in learning was described as requiring the creation of a 'climate of trust' and, particularly in South Africa, the reduction of social tensions. Much of this appeared to revolve around the need to give students choices. A Russian sociology lecturer described how he had developed his lectures with specifically democratic considerations in mind:

> I have reflections on democracy. They perhaps influenced my general attitude towards students and I prefer not to force them into something but to offer them something, starting with [sociological] methods and coming to actual knowledge of concepts. In many lectures I end up with open questions so I show them a different approach and I don't say that this is the best and this is the worst ... this is up to you.

Now this might not seem to be an unusually radical transformation of teaching methods within the humanities. Students of sociology might normally be expected to make their own judgements in the light of competing claims. One should bear in mind, however, that this lecturer was teaching in a country where sociological debate had, until recently, only been encouraged where it could be seen to reinforce a particular political perspective. In fact, he told me, the existence of a sociology department in a Russian university was only legalized in the late 1980s.

Encouraging students to exercise judgement in their choice of perspective within the discipline supports democratic relationships. Others emphasized the value of students having some element of choice in the teaching methods used. A Russian lecturer 'ask(s) them is it okay to use small group methods. I describe it, and they can say yes or no'.

To a large extent the teachers' strategies reflected the kinds of relationship with the students that the lecturer was aiming for. Here, a black South African woman describes her approach as a reaction to the authoritarian relations of apartheid:

> I grew up in the world of being timid, speaking when you are spoken to, being told 'do this', and if you have not been told, you don't do it. So what I try to push into my students' behaviour is that they query things, ask questions, that's why sometimes I say something totally controversial because I am shocking them back into life.

While many lecturers might want to reject the traditional methods that they suffered as students as being ineffective, for this lecturer the 'world of being timid' clearly refers to experience of oppression that extends beyond the classroom. She develops strategies in order to contribute to a more democratic world for her students – this, despite a claim she made earlier in the interview that she was 'not into politics'.

The curriculum and democracy

Most of the South African and Russian lecturers talked about how the content as well as the process of their teaching was shaped by democratic considerations. The clearest cases were in Russia where the demise of communism led to the birth of sociology departments and the changing content of the curriculum was seen by several (in the humanities) to be more significant than changes in teaching processes. The freedom that students now have to discuss politics impacts upon both the process and the content of the lecturers' teaching.

A South African lecturer described how process and content come together in a curriculum that takes the development of multicultural identity in the new democracy seriously: 'We have modules dealing with multilingual education, first and second language teaching, but also the way in which the course is delivered is attempting to develop a dialogue between students who may not have previously had that dialogue with each other.'

He felt, however, that there was a danger where issues of social awareness were 'foisted on [students] by curriculum designers'. A British lecturer in the arts referred to a similar problem where the social values of the subject were 'packaged off into a unit', thereby failing to integrate such issues into the mainstream of the subject. This idea that professional, political or social values can be 'bolted on' to traditional knowledge-based curricula was identified by several British lecturers as being a problem with modularization. It reflects a positivist view of knowledge that treats questions of fact and questions of value as if they can be addressed separately.

Several lecturers in each country articulated ways in which they attempted to reconceive their particular subject in the light of social and democratic considerations.

A British landscape architect, for example, reconceived the subject in terms of 'a social model' informed by purposes and values with which she identifies. Such values connect directly with how she views society. A Russian biologist rejects the traditional biological premise of 'a man as king of a nation and only man is on the top of the ecological mountain'. For her, biology should instead be founded upon a much more organic world-view, and she attempts to reflect this in her curriculum. A South African physicist talked about changing his subject away from an elitist view of physics towards one that is 'about the real world' of ordinary people. Such changes reflect the lecturers' personal values which also inform their aspirations for society, even where these social values are not understood primarily in terms of democracy.

In talking about their teaching, the British lecturers used the term 'democracy' much less frequently than their Russian and South African counterparts. This could be because the political changes in Britain have been different from those in Russia and South Africa. Perhaps democracy was simply not such an important issue for them. Or it could be that the term 'democracy' plays a less central role in political discourse in the UK; or that it has now lost its radical connotations. Many of the British lecturers did, however, make reference to modularization of the curriculum as being largely hostile to their social, as well as academic aims.

Typically, one described how, with modularization, 'what happened with our courses was that things were packaged and compartmentalized and so students see this series of sort of fragmented things, when one of the most important things about the discipline is that you relate all the different parts and integrate different parts'.

Other British lecturers described how fragmentation resulting from modularization militated against interdisciplinary understanding, as suggested in the previous chapter. According to a science lecturer, it did nothing to counter how 'scientists all too often ignore the deep philosophical and sociological questions raised by some of what they are getting into'. Blindness to ethical considerations on the part of science has been held by many to pose a threat to the development of democracy.

Another described how 'packaged into miserable short chunks' it allowed students 'to very easily adopt an attitude of great dependency' and 'rewards competitiveness rather than cooperation'. Several described modularization, in similarly pejorative terms, as a feature of the 'marketized' curriculum.

The influence of what were variously termed 'marketization', 'globalization', 'Americanization' or – as one South African lecturer more colourfully put it – 'the Coca Cola society' was a prominent theme in the interviews in all three countries. It appeared to mark a point at which lecturers saw their own educational values to be in stark contrast to those of their students. In terms of the argument of the last chapter, it appeared that the demands for compliance to the needs of the global market characterized the students' perspective, while the development of critique and contestation reflected the values of the lecturers.

Lecturers' values and their perceptions of their students

Discussion of democracy and social change inevitably reflects the speakers' values. Many lecturers in all three countries spoke critically of their students as variously 'apolitical', 'apathetic', 'instrumental', 'consumerist', 'competitive', 'calculating', 'pragmatic' and 'job-oriented'. Two Russians referred to students becoming 'less passionate', a particularly significant expression in the light of the Russian cultural and literary tradition in which the 'passionate intellectual' is so prominent. In these ways, lecturers in all countries seemed to see their students as having taken on the values of the free market that they, largely, rejected.

While many lecturers appeared to blame the students for holding these values, a few wanted to consider the issue more deeply. 'I am not saying that they are not as politically aware but I think their goals and their motivation are very different. That's my very strong sense,' according to a South African. A British lecturer went further to try to account for apparent student apathy:

> I don't think students have necessarily changed, I think it's more to do with the institution changing: this thing about marketable skills, and so on ... I perceive students as being not particularly interested in what I'd call radical issues based around equality or whatever ... maybe they've got scared of being like that ... but there is a general culture of those things being more marginal.

The Russians' response to the demise of the old certainties of communism – and the rise of the market – was somewhat more ambivalent. Some welcomed the generally more relaxed attitudes, freed from the constraints of communist ideology. They also, however, saw students as being 'confused', 'disoriented' and 'lacking in firm structures'. For them, the well-known quip seemed to apply: 'God is dead, Marxism is undergoing crisis, and I don't feel so well myself' (Eco 1987: 126).

The extent to which lecturers in all three countries expressed their own values to be in conflict with those of their students was particularly significant. They spoke of the importance of 'honesty and kindness', 'colla-boration', 'equality, sharing and sociability' and 'anti-prejudice'. These were the values that, they said, underpinned their teaching, but they felt were often met by opposing values from their students. This presented many with problems in their teaching.

If, as lecturers in all three countries seemed to be claiming, market forces were shaping their students' values towards more individualism and self-interest, how was it that such forces were not, to the same extent, shaping their own values? How accurate were their perceptions of their students? It was not the purpose of this study to go beyond lecturers' views, or to make judgements about those views. However, the single discussion held with a group of students (from Russia) threw an interesting light on the lecturers' perceptions of students' values. Talking about jobs, a student said: 'I think that present students should be more pragmatic because in the past when people studied at universities they studied free of charge, they didn't worry about their future because there was no unemployment and they knew they would have a job ... I wish I was more pragmatic.'

This suggested that while market forces might constitute a pressure towards pragmatism, they do not necessarily adopt it, even though they recognize that it would be in their interests to do so.

Later in the group conversation, a student who claimed that none of them was interested in politics, referred to the current political situation:

Every time we are surprised. Shocked, surprised and wonder what is happening, but I can't say I am interested in politics ... If I start thinking more and more about the political situation I get sadder and more upset ... I think there is no need to bomb Yugoslavia. There is no need. I think the Americans made a big mistake. I think there is an opportunity to say to them to communicate with each other and compromise.

As the conversation went on, other students commented on the increasing gap between the poor and the rich.

These comments suggested a feeling of disillusionment in political sys-tems and disempowerment, and a deep anxiety about the social context, rather than lack of political concern. Perhaps the British and South African lecturers, like their Russian colleagues, may be inclined to misread student disillusionment as reflecting a lack of social concern.

Similarly, the lecturers' common complaint in all three countries that students were 'obsessed with assessment' and only studied 'as a qualification for a job' in response to 'the market' might reflect a stereotype of the student. Such stereotyping might be the result of a tendency for teachers to project onto their students their own frustrations with the social context in which they practise. If so, this would militate against effective communica-tion and therefore teaching.

One British interviewee was concerned to challenge this stereotype: 'This thing about [the students' concern for] marketable skills and knowledge and so on ... if you challenge some of these notions, students are in the main very receptive and interested in learning without regard to a particular job at the end.' She went on to account for the prominence of this stereotype as a response to institutional pressures.

Another British lecturer explained how such pressures did not impact so forcibly upon her, as a relatively junior member of staff:

> I am not very involved at university level ... By and large you are fairly isolated from the university structure, aren't you, working in your little office, going to teach students, come back, interact with postgraduates. Really, what the university wants has very little impact on me. Which probably isn't what the university wants!

Such a viewpoint suggests that the wider forces of globalization and national policy, to which institutions respond, may well have more influence upon students than upon their teachers. Perhaps students cannot so readily isolate themselves from the pragmatic imperatives of a degree course.

This perception of a gap between the lecturers' values and their perceptions of the values of their students was a prominent theme in the interviews. It impacted upon the way lecturers wanted to relate to their students, and wanted their students to relate to each other. Such relationships were often seen in terms of democratic considerations.

Relationships between teachers and students

The British lecturers talked more about their relationships with their students than did their Russian and South African counterparts. Perhaps they had more experience of ways of teaching apart from the lecture format. A wider variety of methods would highlight the importance of student–teacher relationships. Many emphasized their desire for relationships of 'equality' with their students, so that teacher and learner could 'explore together'. While one spoke of an 'inherent inequality' of the teaching relationship, many talked about trying to overcome this teacher–learner power relationship. If there was one theme that drew together nearly all the British lecturers in their thoughts about teaching, it was this concern for equalizing the student–teacher power relationship. Thus, while the term 'democracy' was often not a term they used in connection with their teaching, equality – an important condition for democracy – was of vital importance.

One described how she liked her lessons to be 'noisy': 'I don't like me speaking and them listening and writing. In fact, if they're not talking to me I don't know what they're learning.' She went on to describe how her attempts to support students within an informal relationship could be misread by colleagues once they were taken outside the classroom:

One of my third-year students came to me and I was really busy, but said if we went out and grabbed a sandwich we could talk over lunch, and we went out and got a sandwich and I thought afterwards that probably looked really odd, just having a chat with a third-year student in a café. It's not the sort of thing that goes off very much here. Other staff members don't do it. I thought they are all going to think 'what's she doing with a virile third-year?' But, I mean, it doesn't bother me at all.

The place of such informality and equality of relationship, however, is culturally shaped. A Russian explained how 'we try to establish friendly democratic relationships with the students ... We haven't thought about it, it's just a tradition. As a department we have tea together and we organize friendly barbecues together.' Yet this democratic informality outside the classroom contrasts with their formal tradition in which Russian students stand up as the lecturer enters the auditorium. Lecturers did not necessarily view this tradition as undemocratic. One described the custom as 'a joke', which some lecturers insisted on and others dispensed with. He went on to explain how the tradition symbolized the authority of the discipline itself, rather than the power of the lecturer. This respect for the discipline as the path to truth values knowledge in more than merely commercial terms. Many of my Russian interviewees felt this confidence in the authority of the discipline to be central to the Russian academic tradition, but undermined by marketization.

Cultural traditions were also prominent in some of the South African lecturers' comments. The added complexity here, however, was the range of different traditions amongst the lecturers and students due, in large part, to the diversity of their ethnic identities. Here a black community health lecturer uses her identity to advantage:

> I have a special advantage of being older and also being black. I can get away with things that perhaps a white person wouldn't. It would be offensive. Let's say, for instance, that the problem at the moment in our country is AIDS ... I would say that one of the downfalls of blacks is that they do not want to use a condom because you do not feel as you would if it was flesh to flesh, so I made a joke about it and said 'remember if it is flesh to flesh, then it is dust to dust'. I am getting the message across in a jocular way, which another person of a different colour wouldn't get away with ... They look up to me as their mother.

Laughing as she told me this anecdote, this lecturer was aware of the irony. As a representative of a doubly oppressed group (female, black) she was able to draw upon her traditional power (mother, lecturer) in order to promote the health of blacks, in a way that a white lecturer could not.

A Russian female lecturer commented on how the traditional authority of the mother, which she could draw upon, was not available to the lecturer in an American university she had visited: 'In our country, when I saw students with bad marks I always ask them a thousand questions – "Why don't you go to lectures? What's happened?" – and then I usually punish them like a mother.'

Thus, while relationships with students may be based upon knowledge and values about teaching and learning, or upon a concern for democracy, cultural traditions are also important factors in determining relationships. Changing teaching involves much more than simply learning about new methods.

Some of the British lecturers pointed out the significance of cultural difference when it came to teaching students from certain 'Eastern' (*sic*) countries. One said that these students were much less inclined to collaborate with each other. Explanations for this tendency were expressed in terms of their perceived competitiveness and their belief that only the teacher knew what was worth knowing. Some of these lecturers valued cooperation as a social end in itself. Others emphasized its value on the grounds that 'this led to better work outcomes'.

At times, however, the concern to encourage students to work together was seen in more explicitly social terms. A South African lecturer who described himself as ethnically 'Indian' talked about how it was not just a matter of encouraging Indian and African students to work in mixed-race groups:

> I don't force it [mixed-race groupings]. You see, if I could force an arrangement I'm sure it will happen but, just the way people sit [in their ethnic groupings] it doesn't allow the inter-race thing so much . . . Even amongst the African students or amongst the Indian students people sometimes just don't get on with others . . . Whilst we're concerned about inter-race [collaboration], I mean there's a whole lot of other intra-race things that need to take place as well.

In general the British lecturers talked much more about relationships, particularly those between the students. Many justified collaboration between students in educational terms, and others said this was 'an end in itself'. It seemed that the idea that teaching involves collaboration, questioning from the students and the development of interpersonal skills was a more central part of their thinking than it was for their counterparts. There, perhaps, the lecture format was less challenged.

In their reflections upon their teaching methods, the values that underlay these and the relationships that they aimed to promote, many lecturers from all three countries spoke about the importance of developing critical abilities in their students.

The critical purpose of higher education

The concepts of 'critique' and 'critical thinking' are notoriously difficult to pin down. Democracy is also a concept that appears to have different meanings in different contexts. Several lecturers, however, spoke of students' critical abilities as if they were central to playing a full part in a democratic society, as educational philosophers and sociologists often suggest (see, for example, Carr and Kemmis 1986; Barnett 1997). Many also said they viewed the role of higher education as being concerned with the development of critical abilities. Their views seemed to confirm the argument that if teaching students to become critical is necessary for preparing them for a democratic society, then the idea of 'critique' might be an educational aim that links teaching with its democratic purpose.

A South African lecturer made a clear distinction between 'effective' teaching and the development of critique. She explained that 'effective teaching is effective insofar as students learn what they are supposed to learn', but this does not necessarily contribute to the 'transformation of the country, democracy, social change, empowerment of the poor, addressing issues of poverty'. In order to achieve these things, engineers, for example, would need to be educated in the debates concerning 'what it means to be an engineer in South Africa today'. From her point of view, higher education should engage students with the discipline and its methods, but also help them to integrate that understanding into a wider social world. This twofold purpose reflects the argument of the last chapter, that higher education should both comply with the demands of disciplinary knowledge and also contest its assumptions and transgress its boundaries.

In Russia the idea of being critical was often identified with the new-found freedom to criticize. With that association in mind, one Russian said: 'not everyone can become critical. If everyone started criticizing society there will be trouble.' This might seem to imply that a higher education that develops critical faculties might be all right for an elite, but not for the masses. She went on: 'We are not against this idea that the role of higher education is to develop and to encourage students' critiques, to express their ideas, and skilfully criticize. But it's not the special purpose of higher education, we think.'

In a society where there has been no freedom to criticize, such a freedom is a necessary precondition of democratic living. It is not, however, as many Russians pointed out to me, a sufficient one. While the strength of Russian academic traditions was often referred to, as were the constraints of the Soviet era, the term 'critical' was rarely used in reference to these traditions, but rather to indicate freedom from the Soviet era in which criticism was not permitted.

The South African lecturers were aware that the changes in their society were a result of a political critique of apartheid. Many of them had played an active part in this struggle. They thus saw critique as an instrument of productive social change. Russian lecturers, on the other hand, spoke as if the changes in their society had taken place quite outside their control and irrespective of any critique they might have mounted. For that reason, perhaps, critique was for them not so much a means of effective political engagement as an individual permissive right. It was therefore not so central in their way of thinking about the aims of their professional practice.

For the British lecturers, the idea of critique played a central role in their thinking about their teaching, unlike the Russians. It was not so often talked about in the context of social and cultural change, however, as it was by the South Africans.

We are 'failing in higher education,' said one British lecturer, 'if we do not engender some form of questioning from our students'. He went on to argue, however, that such questioning in society at large is often ill-informed. Critique – or 'well-informed questioning' as he would have it – arises when students are able to see beyond their disciplinary boundaries. 'As a scientist,' he said, 'we are not always encouraged to do that.'

Again, there was a view that a fragmented subject matter, often characteristic of modularization, failed to develop in students the kind of critical thinking that challenges accepted disciplinary boundaries. That kind of thinking was needed, it was claimed, if students are to become questioning adults in a democratic society. Another British science lecturer spoke at length about how he aimed to develop criticality amongst his students. He continued: 'I wouldn't aim to say that I was teaching citizenship', but nevertheless 'I think criticality can make a better citizen.' Reflecting the view of several lecturers concerning recent trends, he said critical abilities were being replaced by more superficial generic skills. While these 'can be more readily written as objectives', such skills cannot readily be translated into critical abilities. While an insistence on clearly definable objectives can help lecturers focus on what they hope to achieve from their teaching, an over-reliance upon them can serve to undermine the critical and therefore the social and political purposes that higher education serves.

Higher education is no doubt a 'critical business', as Barnett (1997) claims. For these lecturers from Russia, South Africa and the UK, however, the term had different significance. The Russians tended to emphasize freedoms, the South Africans emphasized a struggle against inequality, and the British emphasized the intellectual dimension. If the critical purposes of higher education are connected to its democratic function, and given the very different political contexts of the three countries, then we might expect these differing emphases to be reflected in their conceptions of democracy itself.

Changing conceptions of democracy

Russian and South African lecturers more readily introduced the word 'democracy' into the conversation than did the British. In different ways they also saw it as a complex and shifting term that lacks theorization.

For the Russians, now that the Young Communists and other organized youth groups were no longer part of university life for the students, and Marxist–Leninist materialism no longer held a central place in their framework for understanding politics, several respondents pointed out that democracy was an uncertain idea. There was none of the 'solidarity' or 'strong united force' required for democracy, as they understood it. Material conditions contributed to this insecurity. As one of them explained: 'The term democracy is quite complicated. There are different aspects. People have the chance to choose something, to speak, more than we used to before ... [but] if in a democratic society people work and don't receive payment for their work, I rather doubt that it is democracy.'

This comment was particularly poignant in this situation where these Russian academics had often, during the last few years, worked for months on end without being paid. For many in their society, the recent freedoms have led to increased poverty. The class structure of society, I was told, had changed and academics' relative material position had declined considerably. In such circumstances they described Russian democracy as being 'only on paper', where 'the same people have power', and where those with power 'just think about their own profit'.

At the time of the interviews, Western (predominantly British and American) forces were conducting a bombing campaign in Serbia. Noting how this war had been portrayed quite differently on Western television (to which Russians now have access) and Russian television, one respondent concluded that perhaps the Russian media was more open than the British. He was sceptical about the freedom of the press in Russia and the West, however, since 'politicians play with people in the same way and it's difficult to get objective information'.

South African lecturers also expressed uncertainty about the term democracy, reflecting the different social changes that had taken place there. Several expressed the view that their society was more democratic than previously, but now 'people are talking about more mundane things like the delivery of services ... you are talking about a different type of democracy'. Some antagonism was expressed towards growing bureaucracy. As one put it: 'the conservatism ... pragmatics ... language of bureaucracy, control, accountability, all of those sorts of issues, which is a good thing in some ways but the ideology has changed'.

The previous ideology was premised upon opposition to the apartheid rule. This had provided a framework against which democracy could be understood in South Africa, a framework that had also been lacking in Russia since the decline of communism. Now, however, it was becoming more uncertain as the country became more involved in the global economy.

For the British lecturers, social values (and therefore presumably their conceptions of democracy) were couched more in terms of the values of caring, cooperation, equality and lack of prejudice. One person talked about a reduction in prejudice, but several people talked about how such values were undermined by a growing predominance of managerialism, a culture of accountability, assessment and competition. We have seen how modularization was often seen to be part of, or perhaps symbolic of, this trend. Many talked about how these cultural trends impacted negatively upon their teaching and damaged relationships with and amongst students.

A significant proportion of people in each country group, however, did not appear to see discussion of these social and political issues as being central in their thinking about their teaching. One has to be careful, however, in interpreting this denial of interest in politics in a society in which there has been so much disillusionment in what politicians have achieved. A Russian who professed no interest in politics went on to argue coherently about the role of the Russian intellectual in society, drawing on Plato. She was certainly interested in wider social issues, but the term 'politics' is not how she would describe that interest or its relevance to teaching. Perhaps the Russian lecturers, like their students above, were reluctant to describe their interests as 'political' in the light of the negative connotations that the term had for them.

One common thread to emerge from the discussions of democracy was the growth in individualism. Russian and South African lecturers contrasted this with the need for solidarity in a democratic society. The lack of solidarity was associated with a rise of the free market and globalization.

South African and British lecturers talked about educational policy initiatives, which several associated with an environment that is increasingly individualist, competitive and hostile to collaboration. Some, however, pointed out that while policies appeared to be formulated without any educational understanding, they at least put teaching more firmly on the agenda. Although this often led to conformity, it could also, somewhat paradoxically, lead to productive debate. In both countries, however, more criticisms were raised about how such initiatives (involving quality assurance, curriculum reform, etc.) led to conformity and conservatism, rather than development.

While South African and British lecturers talked readily about the policy context of their teaching, the question of educational policy rarely arose in the Russian discussions. This may reflect the fact that educational development has not been a high priority in Russia's policy agenda. Several welcomed the increased openness to the influence of the West in terms of contact with different cultures and widening the curriculum. There appeared to be little awareness, however, of national educational policies associated with the rise of the free market and globalization. In contrast, there was a very much stronger sense of a Russian academic tradition that predates the Leninist revolution. This was upheld by many as a strength that must be preserved in the face of what was variously described as 'the free market', 'globalization', 'Western influence' or, simply, 'the USA'. An element of hopefulness here might be that if this intellectual tradition was able to survive the ravages of Czarism and Communism, perhaps it could survive the worst excesses of globalization.

Discussion and conclusions

The way we understand democracy depends upon our socio-political context. The Russians understood it in terms of the removal of the constraints of the Soviet era; for the South Africans the challenge of creating a multi-cultural post-apartheid society was prominent; while for the British the issue was perhaps more about the threat to the social values of democracy – cooperation, care and critique – which they saw as being threatened by market ideology.

Behind these differences, however, emerged a common theme: globalization. Lecturers almost invariably viewed this trend as being contrary to their academic values. They felt it strongly influenced their students and undermined effective teaching and the promotion of more democratic relationships. Conversation with students, however, suggested that the lecturers' perception of students' values might amount to an unhelpful stereotype.

In this context, and at times in spite of it, nearly all the lecturers attempted to teach using more interactive methods. Most saw these as being more effective, while some saw such methods as directly contributing to the development of democratic citizenship amongst their students. These developments, however, were strongly shaped by the cultural traditions and assumptions that may withstand some of the current influences of globalization.

While effective teaching would seem to be a necessary component of teaching for democracy, it is not a sufficient one. In addition, critical understandings were seen as important, though the term 'critical' appeared to mean different things in the different contexts.

The exploration of this relationship between teaching and democracy has a long history, at least since Plato wrote *The Republic*. More recently, James Dewey – whose educational philosophy has had considerable impact in all three of the countries in this study – made quite specific claims about the relationship between classroom learning, the importance of student autonomy, and the development of democracy, not unlike some of the interviewees. Speaking about the curriculum he said: 'To subject the mind to an outside and ready-made material is a denial of the ideal of democracy, which roots itself ultimately in the principle of moral, self-directing individuality' (Dewey 1941: 68).

This lack of student autonomy relates closely to some of the complaints the British lecturers made about modularization. Here, however, Dewey, unlike the lecturers, makes the link with democracy quite explicit.

There has been a great deal of literature since Dewey's time, which has commented on the ways in which teaching reflects, reproduces, or aims to enhance social and political relationships in the wider society. The vast majority of this, however, relates to schooling. Until recently, little has been written about how higher education teaching relates to concerns for democracy. In an exception to this general trend, Blake's consideration of post-Dearing UK higher education, drawing upon Dewey's ideas about democratic relationships, reflects what many of the lecturers had to say:

> Democracy is founded on faith in the power of 'pooled and co-operative experience'. Through democratic, open relationships, as opposed to autocratic and authoritarian ones, however benign, we learn from and with one another. We can know things in this way, in combination with one another, that we cannot know alone. Unless democratic habits of thought and action are part of 'the fiber of a people', Dewey writes, political democracy is insecure.
>
> (Blake *et al.* 1998: 100)

A study of the UK literature concerned with teaching and learning in higher education has shown that questions about the purposes of higher education, such as its role in democratic society, are almost completely separated from questions about pedagogy (Malcolm and Zukas 2001). Indeed, the literature on the ways in which teaching and learning take place, and the literature that is concerned with the purposes of higher education, typically make no reference to each other's work (Rowland 2000: 5–7).

An influential reviewer of the literature (Entwistle 1992: 10) suggested that the link between teaching and political values, made by such writers as Rogers (1978), is not essential. He claimed that teaching methods in higher education need not be linked with such concerns as the redistribution of power in society. Most of the lecturers in this study saw some linkage and this was a motivation for their teaching. The salient question now seems to be: *should* lecturers be aware of these links? Should an aim of professional development programmes, such as those accredited in the UK by the Higher Education Academy (HEA), be to develop such awareness? In fact, a criterion for such courses receiving HEA accreditation is that they must demonstrate that they develop certain 'professional values'. These include a 'commitment to equality of educational opportunity' (HEA 2004). This is essential, but far short of a commitment to democratic values.

A Russian lecturer opened this chapter by insisting that you 'have to do something' to promote democracy. The argument of the previous chapter, however, suggests that promoting criticality and democracy is in tension with, and may even be undermined by, the current emphasis that is placed upon developing the skills required to serve the needs of a global economy. The next chapter will consider how this might be so and how universities might respond to these demands without undermining their social and intellectual purposes.

4

The skills agenda

I am currently working on my PhD and am learning a variety of new skills such as self-discipline, time management and developing my own initiative.

(PhD student, in UCL 2004)

PhD students are expected to make a substantial, original contribution to knowledge ... The development of wider employment-related skills should not detract from that core objective.

(BBSRC 2001)

Introduction

There is a danger that undue emphasis upon the development of skills to meet the economic needs of society may undermine the critical purposes of academic work. In the tension between compliance and contestation, compliance appears to have the upper hand. If the enquiring university is to provide a critical service to society, it must find ways to engage critically with the society it serves, and thereby serve the society it critiques.

This tension between the intellectual, theoretical and critical purposes of higher education on the one hand and the economic, practical and service purposes on the other is perhaps most keenly felt in relation to what has come to be called 'the skills agenda'. In this chapter I shall explore these tensions, and some of the confusions that have arisen, in an attempt to articulate the need for a language that is more grounded in the sense of enquiry that underlies university work. For, as I shall argue, the language of skills acquisition that is used to represent academic practices fails to give an adequate account of the contribution that higher education makes to society.

Why should the importance of skills raise a particular problem?

Why skills?

A natural starting point might be to try to define some of the terms involved, such as 'learning', 'knowledge', 'skill' and its various categories (such as employment skills, transferable skills, core skills and key skills). Attempts to define and categorize knowledge and skill, however, inevitably lead to tortuous epistemological discussion. 'Learning' means very different things in different contexts and from different disciplinary perspectives (Rowland 2000: 49–51). And attempts to categorize skills lead to problems of a different sort as anyone who has attempted to identify the skills developed on a particular course knows. One of many attempts to provide an overall categorization of skills, for example, identified 108 skills organized into eight categories within four 'zones' (Allen 1993).

The fact that there have been many such attempts suggests that it might be better to start from a different place. Definitions and meanings are not always the best first step in attempting to clarify a concept. The philosopher Wittgenstein opened the first of an important series of lectures with: 'What is the meaning of a word?' (Wittgenstein 1958: 1). While giving no definitional answer, the thrust of his enquiry was to draw attention to the 'language games' we play, as he would put it, rather than to definitions. One would be hard pressed to define 'word', but this difficulty does not impede our satisfactory use of the term in normal circumstances. We are familiar with the language game in which the word 'word' plays its part. When the circumstances are not normal, however (such as when discussing a text in code), we might be led to think about definitions. Similarly, in this discussion of skills, we may need to consider if the particular circumstances in which the term is being used are normal. If not, then the question of definitions is likely to arise.

This suggests that a useful strategy for considering the value and impact of the skills agenda might be to analyse the use to which the term is put in some particular example. This approach should enable me to develop some critical commentary and indicate how we might respond to the imperatives and language of the skills agenda in a more critical and useful way.

Skills for research students

The *Joint Statement of the Research Councils'/AHRB's Skills Training Requirements for Research Students* (BBSRC 2001) is my example.

The reason for choosing this is that it has been prominent in recent postgraduate education developments; that it is a well-known and readily accessible statement with considerable authority amongst those involved in postgraduate education in the UK; and that its focus on research students is informative of the ways in which research as well as teaching are addressed.

For the skills agenda now impacts not only upon teaching but also upon research.

Another reason for selecting this document is that it is concerned specifically with the development of the research student as a researcher rather than as an employee in any more general sense. The impact of the skills agenda upon the academic objectives of PhD study is of concern here, rather than the question of whether there are other specifically employment-related objectives that PhD study might meet.

This document lists a number of skills in various categories: Research Skills and Techniques, Research Environment, Research Management, Personal Effectiveness, Communication Skills, Networking and Teamworking, and finally Career Management. The list is intended to help universities maintain research training 'of the highest standard, across all disciplines' (BBSRC 2001: 1). Under 'Research Skills and Techniques' appears the following list of skills that should be expected of the typical research student and therefore should be borne in mind in their training programmes:

(A) Research Skills and Techniques – to be able to demonstrate:

1. the ability to recognise and validate problems
2. original, independent and critical thinking, and the ability to develop theoretical concepts
3. a knowledge of recent advances within one's field and in related areas
4. an understanding of relevant research methodologies and techniques and their appropriate application within one's research field
5. the ability to critically analyse and evaluate one's findings and those of others
6. an ability to summarise, document, report and reflect on progress.

(BBSRC 2001: 2)

It is difficult to envisage someone completing a PhD without having some ability in these respects. One is struck, however, by the phrase 'to be able to demonstrate' that precedes each item. Lists of skills often start with such verbs to indicate skills or procedural knowledge rather than propositional knowledge. The distinction often made here is between knowing *that* and knowing *how* (Eraut 1994, drawing on Ryle 1949). Three of the items, however, then start with the word 'ability'. The implication seems to be that the ability (to summarize, for example) is not the issue but rather the ability to demonstrate that ability. But what would it be for someone to have the ability to summarize without being able to demonstrate it in some way? Of course, one might be temporarily incapacitated; or one may not wish to demonstrate it; or physical conditions may at any time prevent one from demonstrating it; or one may simply not be required to demonstrate it. There are not two separate activities that a student may be able to perform:

summarizing and demonstrating the ability to summarize. One is doing the latter by virtue of doing the former. It is not as if there were some mental state called 'the ability to summarize' – a kind of Cartesian ghost in the machine – which may, or may not, be accompanied by the (physical/behavioural) ability to demonstrate it. This kind of point was often made by the philosopher Gilbert Ryle (Ryle 1949), who was concerned to eradicate the Cartesian separation of mind and body.

In the three cases where students are expected 'to be able to demonstrate the ability to' do something, the least we can say is that this is an unusual use of language. Such unusual usage naturally leads one to reconsider what might be meant by 'skill' here and why language is being used in this striking way.

Of course, research students often have abilities that they are reluctant to demonstrate. Perhaps students are able to summarize what they have read, but are reluctant to show their summary to their supervisor or their fellow students for fear of being criticized. It is quite proper that postgraduate studies should help students overcome such fears. Furthermore, students may be able to make such summaries for themselves but not be able to communicate them effectively to others. The development of such an ability (a 'communication skill', if you will) might also form part of a research programme. But these personal, social and communication skills would not come under the heading of 'Research Skills and Techniques'. Indeed, the document goes on to list such communication skills.

There thus seem to be two possible interpretations: either the term 'skill' is being used in a very special sense in which it may be possible to have it without being able to act upon it; or else the skill in question is actually a *demonstration* skill.

The other three items in the list refer to particular kinds of thinking (item 2), knowledge (3) and understanding (4). Again, these are preceded by the phrase 'to be able to demonstrate'. There are some psychologists, like de Bono (1982), who would argue that 'critical thinking' (in item 2) is a skill, or set of skills, or procedure, that can be applied across a wide range of contexts as seems to be implied by this list. Much psychological research, however, has suggested that, if 'critical thinking' is a skill or a kind of expertise, it is not one that can readily transfer from one field to another (Glaser and Chi 1988: xv–xxviii). On the other hand, one might, like Barnett, view critical thought as a sociological rather than psychological construct. From this point of view critical thinking is not so much a 'set of skills' but rather 'a critical capacity oriented to the world of knowledge' (Barnett 1997: 71).

The ability to demonstrate knowledge, however, *qua* ability, might look like a skill. The question here, though, is how does 'the ability to demonstrate knowledge of relevant advances ...' differ from simply having that knowledge? It could be that the problem the research councils have in mind here is that well-qualified students sometimes appear to have a lot of knowledge without being able to apply it in other contexts. But if that is the case, the solution would not be to develop 'application skills' but to change the focus of the PhD study itself towards a more applied orientation.

Thus, as with the 'abilities' identified in this list, the references to knowledge and understanding also appear to privilege the ability to demonstrate. It is this feature to which the statement of research skills and techniques draws specific attention. Since the PhD thesis provides the natural context for making this demonstration, why does further attention need to be drawn to students' demonstrating abilities?

Performativity and the market

The emphasis upon demonstration is central to the concept of performativity. Lyotard (1984) argues that performativity is the generalized spirit of knowledge in the post-modern age. Many writers since have commented upon how regimes of accountability for teaching and research tend to lead universities to see their work in terms of performance to be assessed and assured. It is performance, or demonstration in this case, rather than the goal of truth, that 'legitimates' the student's knowledge. The implications of this are far reaching for how we are to understand research (let alone research skills). Whereas the PhD has traditionally been judged in terms of one major criterion – that it should constitute a contribution to knowledge – it is now recast in terms of performance. But more importantly, this new emphasis might indicate that whereas the motivation for studying a PhD was traditionally an intrinsic interest in the subject of study, now an instrumental interest in developing one's skills – one's ability to perform – may come to be seen as more important.

As the number of PhD students increases, they come under increasing pressure to improve their abilities to market themselves to their future employers. In the foreword to the Higher Education Funding Council for England's consultation document *Improving Standards in Postgraduate Research Degree Programmes*, the chief conclusion of several recent reviews was held to be:

> the perception that UK research degrees do not prepare people adequately for careers outside academia, either because of insufficient access to transferable skills training, or a more general lack of awareness and articulation among students of the skills gained by studying for a research degree.
>
> (HEFCE 2003: 11)

The claim is that a thesis and its associated *viva voce* examination are no longer an adequate 'articulation ... of the skills gained by studying for a research degree'. What is needed is a more explicit demonstration of skill. In order to achieve this, the 'skills' need to be separable from the context of research in which they were originally expressed. Thus separated, they become valuable commodities or, as Bleakley (2001: 114) puts it, 'an investment or addition to your portfolio of skills and abilities' to take to the market place.

By drawing attention to performance in a statement specifically concerned with 'research skills and techniques', attention is taken away from the central concern of the research student, that is, to make a contribution to knowledge. It is thus not surprising that the Research Councils were anxious that their statement should not 'detract from that core objective' (BBSRC 2001: 1). Presented in this way it is bound to.

In order to avoid these problems the statement could be redrafted as follows:

(A) In the course of their research students will:

1. recognize and validate problems
2. think originally, independently and critically, and develop theoretical concepts
3. know of recent advances within their field and in related areas
4. understand relevant research methodologies and techniques and their appropriate application within the research field
5. critically analyse and evaluate their findings and those of others
6. summarize, document, report and reflect on progress.

In this form, the list includes all of the substantial content of the original. It draws our attention to these aspects of PhD work. Its thrust, however, is quite different. It is no longer a list of skills (or learning outcomes) that the student possesses as a consequence of PhD training, but rather a list of practices that are involved in the process of preparing a research thesis. It is also more demanding. Students no longer simply have to have the ability to do these things, or the ability to demonstrate that they have the ability to do them. The emphasis is now where it should be, upon the serious business of contributing to knowledge by means of a thesis. The problem, however, is that such a list does not explicitly identify what the student will be able to take (as 'outcomes') to the market place as a consequence of study. It does not carry with it an assumption (and a dubious one at that) that such practices can be unproblematically transferred into a different practice as an employee.

I have not commented on the particular abilities that have been chosen for this list. Taken out of any context of knowledge, such skills are inevitably somewhat banal. One does not have to be a PhD student in order to be able to 'recognize problems' or 'evaluate one's findings'. Within their more limited sphere of knowledge, even primary school children have been shown, by very detailed observations of their classroom activity, to do these things very effectively (e.g. Armstrong 1980). If such terms are to fulfil their intended purpose of helping maintain standards of research training, it is difficult to see how they could do so.

Personal skills

While research skills, expressed with this degree of generality, communicate little that relates specifically to the rigours of research within any particular discipline, one might expect that they are little different from the personal qualities that research students bring to bear upon their study. It is therefore interesting to compare the above list with the list under the heading of 'Personal Effectiveness':

(D) Personal Effectiveness – to be able to:

1. demonstrate a willingness and ability to learn and acquire knowledge
2. be creative, innovative and original in one's approach to research
3. demonstrate flexibility and open-mindedness
4. demonstrate self-awareness and the ability to identify own training needs
5. demonstrate self-discipline, motivation, and thoroughness
6. recognise boundaries and draw upon/use sources of support as appropriate
7. show initiative, work independently and be self-reliant

(BBSRC 2001: 3)

Again, the ability to demonstrate is paramount, indicating that in personal matters, as well as academic ones, the emphasis is upon the students' abilities to present and re-present themselves. This continuing emphasis reinforces a view of 'self' that is to be constructed, managed and re-presented.

Leaving aside this issue, it is difficult to see the basis upon which abilities listed under Personal Effectiveness differ from those under Research Skills and Techniques. For example, the ability 'to demonstrate original thinking' appears as a research skill (item 2 in list A), whereas the ability 'to be original in one's approach to research' is an element of personal effectiveness (item 2, list D). While the two statements do not have exactly the same meaning, it is not at all clear how they differ. Similarly, the ability to demonstrate independent thinking appears in one list while the ability to work independently appears in the other. On further inspection, it is difficult to see upon what basis many of the items appear in one list rather than the other. Lists of skills (or learning outcomes) often present this kind of problem. This is because lists are remarkably imprecise ways of representing complex overlapping practices. They inevitably provide a weak (rather than rich) description of practice and if used as a template in, say, a research training course, tend to weaken rather enrich the practice to which they are applied.

A 'willingness to learn' is an example of a skill which, if meaningful, would surely apply to any list of skills related to any area of activity. It is the first item on this list. It is difficult to envisage an area of practice (such as 'management' or 'teamwork', for which the Statement includes other lists of skills) for which a willingness to learn is not a prerequisite of its effective development. Presumably, such willingness also has to be accompanied by an ability to learn. The Dearing Report on Higher Education (an influential document on higher education policy in the UK) identified 'Learning how to learn' as one of the four key skills of the successful graduate (NCIHE 1997: 9.18).

It is, however, difficult to see what meaning to attach to such a key skill. Are we to suppose that someone who has learnt how to learn, and is willing to learn, can apply this skill equally to learning how to play football and learning how to solve quadratic equations? And conversely, how does the infant learn how to speak (arguably one of the most difficult things any human learns) without the benefits of having already developed this key skill? Again, stripped of context, the term 'skill' becomes meaningless.

The purpose of this Joint Statement is to maintain standards. If 'willingness to learn' is indeed a skill, it could only be useful in this regard if it were possible to differentiate between students' possession of the skill. Of course, some students are more willing to learn their subject than others. Some are more willing to learn academically in general than others, perhaps. But to say that some students are unwilling to learn *in general* is odd. It is difficult to conceive of what evidence could be brought to bear upon such a claim.

When the term 'willingness to learn' is used in normal circumstances, the context is assumed in relation to some particular domain of practice or field of knowledge. The student needs to understand that such willingness may be severely tested in relation to his or her field of research in the difficult and challenging business of doing a PhD. Indeed, an interview for a place may well have the identification of the student's willingness, in the context of the field to be studied, as its main objective. Is the student willing to learn in relation to a wide range of ideas related to the field, or is this willingness bounded by a narrower set of interests? Is the student willing to learn about the theoretical and philosophical underpinning of his or her work or more willing to explore practical applications? But to suppose from this that such willingness (or the ability to demonstrate such willingness) is a skill that can be abstracted from any context is absurd.

The question we should be concerned with is not 'is the student able to demonstrate a willingness to learn?' in general, but 'is the student willing to learn in the field relevant to this course of study or research?' In the discussion of the list of research skills I suggested that skills are not necessarily transferable. But here the question 'is this student willing to learn *in general*?' is not one that is open to empirical investigation regarding its transferability because it is not a meaningful question. It lacks conceptual clarity. It represents what Ryle (1949) would have called a 'category error'. It confuses a question of motivation with one of skill. Motivation, of its nature, is motivation towards a goal and therefore, by definition, not separable (transferable) from the goal towards which it is directed.

Of course the 'ability to *demonstrate* a willingness' may be a skill like 'an ability to demonstrate motivation', which also appears on this list. But now the issue is one of demonstration skills, which have already been addressed.

While willingness is not a skill, there is a different sense in which 'willingness to learn' might apply to a wide range of activity. This is in the sense of compliance: the will of the student is directed towards pleasing the teacher, whatever the teacher demands. Education systems readily produce students who perform in this way in the context of their academic work. In fact, in PhD supervision, students' learnt willingness to please and conform can be the biggest block to their developing ability to critique the work of others. It presents a problem for the student who is also expected to be independent, creative, innovative and original.

Such qualities are identified in the second item on this list. Like flexibility and open-mindedness (item 3), self-discipline and motivation (item 5) and initiative, independence and self-reliance (item 7), creativity, innovativeness and originality are important qualities. But it is difficult to see what they have to do with doing a PhD, or conducting research, rather than almost any other professional activity. Thus the student quoted at the head of this chapter, who comments that he has learnt the skills of self-discipline, time management and developing his own initiative, reflects a somewhat dismal view of PhD study. The enormous expense of PhD study is unlikely to be justified on the grounds of producing skills of this order. If such objectives are a priority, there are much more economical ways of meeting them.

Perhaps a statement of the significance of some personal qualities, however, does need to be made in the context of PhD study today. Universities are required to raise completion rates and reduce completion times. Many students, especially in the sciences, conduct their PhD studies within research programmes tightly framed by others. Staff and students are encouraged to view the PhD as preparation for employment and to develop skills appropriate to that end. With pressures such as these, which is the context that this Joint Statement addresses, there is a temptation to push students through their PhDs in ways that restrict the potential for innovation, initiative and creativity. Cramming for a PhD may not be far away. We can see the same pressures on research projects in general. Under such circumstances the personal qualities that constitute an independence of mind, which are essential if university research is to play its critical role, may become undervalued in the face of a demand for compliance with targets. There does need to be careful thought about how critical abilities might be identified and fostered.

Of greater value than lists of skills might be more grounded accounts, or stories, of the practices of exemplar graduate students, with the aim of investigating and articulating their particular value. Holmes (1998) develops this idea in relation to undergraduate education. One might similarly envisage that close accounts of postgraduate practice would go a long way towards developing an understanding of the processes of postgraduate education. The development of such understanding is a precondition for making the kind of judgements that are needed if standards are to be enhanced. Such accounts would also help universities to open up these practices to the wider world, including employers. Something much closer to the lived experience of students than lists of skills is required.

The moral dimension

Another problem which emerges in several items in both the above lists of generic abilities is a confusion between a matter of 'skill' and a matter of 'being'. The 'personal effectiveness' list includes notions such as willingness, motivation and thoroughness; the 'research skills' list includes criticality. Even if we are to concede that the ability to demonstrate such qualities is a skill, the much more important issue is whether or not the student (or employee) actually exercises these abilities.

Barnett (1997) argues, in relation to criticality, that higher education should develop critical 'being' as well as critical thinking. Critical being is not simply a question of being able to demonstrate an ability to think critically, but of having a propensity to *be* critical in relation to knowledge, one's self and the world in general.

If such a quality is viewed simply as a skill which may or may not be deployed, then higher education will be in danger of producing students with a 'truncated sense of critical being ... critical sufficient to keep the corporate organization afloat' (Barnett 1997: 76), but not sufficient to meet the requirement of critical service to society as a whole.

This argument can be extended in relation to skills in general. An education that aims to prepare students to contribute to a better world is, by virtue of that aim, a moral activity. To understand skills in terms that are abstracted from any context, and thus from any judgement that is made regarding their deployment in that context, is a 'truncated' form of education, sufficient, perhaps, for servility, but not for critical service.

My analysis of this particular example suggests that there are serious problems in the application of the skills agenda to postgraduate studies. It lacks coherence and clarity, and promotes an instrumental approach to studies. But in order to appreciate the significance of these problems, we need to view the skills agenda in the much wider context of institutionalized education as a whole. I shall therefore provide a very brief historical account to show how and why the skills agenda has come to impact upon this aspect of university work.

Skills in schools

The emphasis upon skills in education in the UK came to the fore in the early 1980s in the secondary schools and further education sectors; attention was later focused on undergraduate higher education; and more recently, discussions have become prominent in relation to postgraduate and research degrees. While a similar movement has taken place in other countries, it is worth outlining this development in the UK briefly in order to understand the roots of the problems identified in relation to post-graduate study.

In 1982 the Technical and Vocational Education Initiative (TVEI) was announced by the Department for Education and Employment (DfEE), to provide funding for secondary schools in order to 'enable [young people] to be effective, enterprising and capable at work' (Devine *et al.* 1994: 2). The initiative's title and its aim suggest that its purpose was primarily, if not exclusively, directed towards education as a preparation for employment. The initiative was interpreted, however, and its effects came to be seen, in much wider educational terms. Thus, while the DfEE defined its objectives in purely vocational terms, its account of the benefits of taking part included the promotion of positive attitudes to learning in general (DfEE 1996).

Positive attitudes to learning are clearly needed if education is to prepare students for the world of work. But positive attitudes equally serve other educational purposes. They have as much to do with the world of knowledge creation, or with the development of a more just society, or with the personal development of students as they do with the world of work. Indeed, some have claimed that the positive attitudes to learning promoted by TVEI and similar projects in the USA, with their emphasis upon skills development and enterprise, contributed to a process of democratization of the curriculum (Luby 1995). Others, however, saw such government initiatives as an imposed imperative that undermined professional democracy amongst teachers (Kushner 2004). From these early stages the skills agenda was variously interpreted as supporting or undermining the kinds of democratic relations in teaching that were discussed in the last chapter.

One of the means by which benefits were to be accrued, it was argued, was through 'active' approaches to learning. Drawing upon what came to be called 'progressivism' in primary schools of the 1970s, TVEI projects in secondary schools were concerned to develop approaches that were problem-based, student-centred and, in general, moved away from didactic approaches to teaching (Yeomans 1996). In fact, many of the terms that higher education has adopted in the UK to reflect new approaches to teaching and learning have their origins in TVEI and similar initiatives of the 1980s which emphasized the importance of skills.

Thus, even in its early stages in the secondary school sector, the emphasis upon skills was prompted by two quite different concerns. The first was a political judgement that education should serve economic needs. The second was a pedagogical judgement that teaching would be improved by placing a greater emphasis upon skills.

Skills at university

The political and pedagogical aspects of the TVEI were taken forward into the university sector through the Enterprise in Higher Education (EHE) initiative, begun in 1987 (ED 1989). Again, directed at preparing students for employment, the initiative also focused attention on methods of teaching. But whereas secondary school teachers were trained to teach and saw teaching as their central professional practice, this was not normally the case for university teachers at that time. Much of the funding from the EHE initiative was therefore directed towards raising awareness of the importance of university teaching, drawing attention to 'new' methods and supporting the professional development of academic staff. Only by taking university teaching more seriously would students become adequately prepared for the world of work.

This attempt to align higher education more closely with the perceived needs of employers for a highly skilled workforce was associated with a concern to enhance and provide external assurance of the quality of teaching. Some, such as Bridges (1992), valuing the new emphasis upon teaching, saw these developments as being at least consistent with the intellectual purposes of the university. Others, however, were despondent about them being directed towards 'practical life and work skills' (Leftwich 1991) rather than any more intellectually grounded priorities.

EHE funding was used to provide posts, and even whole units, in educational development, and a range of programmes for staff. In one university, it supported what was believed to be the first full Masters course in the UK designed specifically to enhance the quality of teaching across the university (Rowland and Barton 1994). In this instance, the tension between the quality-assured skills-oriented agenda and the growing attention to teaching was notable. In his foreword to a publication of writings by the first participants on this Masters course, the Chair of the Board of Directors of the UK Universities' and Colleges' Staff Development Agency (which funded the publication) stated:

> It is paradoxical that some of the content [of this publication] is critical of current approaches to external quality assurance since one wonders whether the HE community would ever have had the valuable opportunity of these insights and ideas, had such external imperatives never existed.
>
> (Cowell 1995)

Since EHE, it has become commonplace for change and development in university teaching to be led (and often funded) by 'external imperatives'. The paradox, as Cowell calls it, arises when the critical practice of developing teaching takes place in a context of compliance with external imperatives. Such critical compliance is becoming characteristic of the way academic staff comply with external imperatives with some foreboding, but later attempt to use the opportunity (and often the funding) to reinterpret the requirements in terms that suit their more academic concerns.

The emphasis upon the importance of skills has now moved 'up' the system to postgraduate education. UK research councils issued the Joint Statement (BBSRC 2001) examined above. This reflected the research councils' concern to promote 'best practice' in research supervision. While it provided a statement of skills required to support learning (or rather, training) of postgraduate research students, it did not specifically identify the economic purposes that might be served by enhancing postgraduate education. It was followed, however, by the government-commissioned Roberts Review, submitted to the Treasury in order to secure additional funding for postgraduate education. For this reason, it viewed postgraduate education with specific reference to the 'future survival and growth of businesses operating in what are increasingly competitive global markets' (Roberts 2002: 1). Taken together, these influential reports, like the earlier EHE and TVEI initiatives, make specifically pedagogical judgements about the importance of skills training with the purpose of serving specifically economic purposes.

The potential for tension between these educational and economic objectives in postgraduate research was acknowledged in the Joint Statement's concern that the employment-related objectives should not detract from the PhD student's primary aim 'to make a substantial, original contribution to knowledge' (BBSRC 2001: 1). My analysis suggests that their fear was well founded.

The recommendations of these reports were largely incorporated into a code of practice for the quality assurance of research degree programmes developed by the Quality Assurance Agency for Higher Education (QAAHE 2004). With reference to 'research-related', 'employment-related', 'transferable' and 'other appropriate' skills, this code of practice completes a movement of the skills agenda throughout the schools and university sectors of education, together with a means of assuring its implementation. As with the TVEI initiative in schools, it presents skills development both in terms of meeting employment needs and also of 'enabling students to take ownership and responsibility for their own learning' (QAAHE 2004: 20). In combining this economic purpose with a particular view of student learning, what is not so clear is whether by taking 'responsibility for their own learning' students will in fact develop in ways that are in line with employers' needs (however understood). In fact, this seems to be an article of faith behind all of these developments. Presumably, the assumption is that the force of the competitive employment market will impel students to exercise their responsibility for their learning in ways that are directed towards securing improved employment prospects.

Conclusions

This historical résumé of the development of the skills agenda in the UK indicates the need for the enquiring university to work creatively within the tension between the service and critical purposes of academic practices. The preoccupation with documenting lists of skills, however, does not achieve this for several reasons.

The foremost of these concerns the impact that the skills agenda is having upon language. It is ironic that while PhD students are required to be rigorous, clear, precise and insightful, these qualities are signally lacking in a document intended to raise educational standards. The academic community needs to develop its capacity to tell its story in ways that make sense to itself and to the wider community, and this is an aim of this book. The language in which skills are typically addressed, however, is not a promising start. Academic staff and managers have a difficult responsibility here: to respond to the imperatives of the skills agenda in a language that is clear and truthful. As the 'newspeak' of Orwell's *1984* so aptly illustrates, once external imperatives are permitted to distort our language, the ability to think critically is doomed.

Second: somewhat spurious distinctions between knowledge and skills, and a belief that the latter should receive more emphasis, leads to attention being directed towards students' abilities to demonstrate, present and represent themselves. The 'self' then becomes something to be managed for instrumental purposes. Such instrumentality flies in the face of the qualities of 'passion', 'integrity', 'enthusiasm' and 'openness' that the employer, quoted in Chapter 1, was hoping to find in graduate employees. Such qualities will be explored within a different framework in Chapter 8. As we saw in the last chapter, many university teachers already view their students as being too 'instrumental', 'consumerist', 'competitive', 'calculating', 'pragmatic' and 'job-oriented' in their approach to their studies. The skills agenda applied to postgraduate studies is likely to exacerbate this problem. In their dealings with students, it is important that academics emphasize the intrinsic values of curiosity and a thirst for knowledge.

Third: such lists are premised upon untested (and often implausible) assumptions regarding the transferability of skills from one domain to another. These assumptions need to be challenged and examined at all levels of the design and implementation of training programmes.

Fourth: if the value of postgraduate study is seen in terms of the development of such 'skills', this detracts from the central purpose of the PhD as a contribution to knowledge. It also raises the question of whether postgraduate study is in fact the best or most economical way of developing such skills. Universities are in danger of underselling themselves by emphasizing the development of skills that can more economically (and usefully) be developed in other contexts, such as work experience or voluntary service.

Finally, generalized skills (often defined in such terms as key, core, generic or transferable) are often rendered almost meaningless by being identified out of context. They are thus difficult to place into categories or identify with specific practices. As a consequence such generalized lists do not help in making judgements about students' abilities to complete a PhD. Nor do they help in the measurement of student achievement. Instead, the value of PhD study and its articulation needs to be based upon grounded accounts of practice that allow for meaningful critique and development of the ways in which PhD study is supported.

A major source of these difficulties arises from a perceived separation between knowledge and skill, knowing and doing, or theory and practice. This has deep roots in British (as opposed to, for example, Germanic) thinking. While academic practices have traditionally privileged the theoretical, the skills agenda might be seen as an attempt to redress this balance, giving greater emphasis to the practice and application of ideas. Such a change of emphasis is in tune with a greater vocational and employment orientation in education. It may also be appropriate if universities are to engage with the wider community they critically serve. But the poorly conceptualized ways in which the skills agenda has developed fails to give an adequate articulation of the practices, outcomes and purposes of higher education and thus risks lowering the very standards that it seeks to raise. It also serves to fragment further practice from theory, thereby exacerbating the very problem it aimed to address.

This is only a part of a wider fragmentation within the academic community and its practices. In the next chapter I turn to these wider aspects of fragmentation and how they affect the contexts of teaching, learning and research. For it is this fragmentation that provides the challenges that educational and academic development must meet if the university is to provide a critical service to the wider community.

5

Fragmentation in academic life

Introduction

The higher education system lacks confidence in itself and lacks the confidence of the wider society. The sector, especially in the UK, has reluctantly complied with external demands placed upon it to raise and measure its outputs, standardize its practices and submit itself to managerial control with diminished resources and in an increasingly competitive market. This has taken its toll on academic staff. A report commissioned by the UK Association of University Teachers in 2004 found that 69 per cent of academic and academic-related staff agreed strongly with the statement 'I find my job stressful', a figure little changed since 1998 (Kinman and Jones 2004).

But there is another story. The same report also concluded that staff found many aspects of their jobs to be highly rewarding and worthwhile. It found nothing to suggest that the core academic activities of teaching and research are not still enjoyed by most academics.

In this chapter I shall suggest that the fragmentation of academic life, which operates at many levels, may explain the apparently contradictory perception that the academic community is burdened by stress and pressure while, at the same time, its staff are enthusiastic about teaching and research. I shall also argue that the primary focus of academic development should be to build upon this enthusiasm by addressing this fragmentation and restoring the integrity of the professional community. In this way universities will be able to present a more coherent story of their work to themselves and to the wider society.

In the last chapter I illustrated how an emphasis upon skills development can lead to separation between knowledge and skills (and theory and practice) in relation to postgraduate research. The same dangers apply to such a direct skills-based approach in relation to teaching and research more generally, and to management and other academic practices. The development of skills is, of course, important. But when considered in isolation from the wider contexts and purposes to which they might be directed, an explicit focus upon skills can fragment and undermine the integrity of academic work. My argument is therefore at odds with the dominant view that skills (especially in relation to teaching, but increasingly in terms of management as well) should be a direct focus for development.

By addressing the fragmentation of university life I hope to show the kind of space in which academic development needs to work. The nature of this work will then be the subject of the subsequent chapter.

The problem of fragmentation

Fragmentation is not peculiar to universities. In the UK we have recently been made aware of the consequences of fragmentation in the rail industry, in the medical world and in other areas of professional life and public services. An almost trivial story, reported in the UK national press (Radnedge 2005), of a Nigerian schoolgirl who saved a large train company £250,000 simply by making detailed observations of trains that started late because of cleaning and safety checks, illustrates the point. In this case the fragmentation between train operators, drivers and maintenance staff led to lack of communication and confusions about responsibilities which undermined the effectiveness of the organization as a whole. It reflects the larger story of the British railway system which, following privatization, was split into different units. This led to a failure to deal adequately with the conflicting demands of safety and punctuality. Perhaps this could be a lesson for the institutions of higher education. For even though there is broad agreement that different areas of higher education practice should work in harness, in fact staff juggle with the experience of teaching, research and management pulling in conflicting directions.

The wider trend in society towards fragmentation can be understood as a consequence of globalization and market forces; or as a feature of a postmodern world in which there is little in the way of shared beliefs to hold society together; or in terms of the need of capital to create a new economic order to advance its interests; or as a consequence of advances in technology and knowledge which make communication almost instant and thereby collapse our sense of space and time. Or we could view fragmentation in professional life as simply a result of the failure to respond appropriately or professionally to all of these.

Much has been written about the fragmentation of society and communities within it. Here I shall only attempt to portray the fragmentation that characterizes higher education in particular, rather than theorize how it might be related to the more general conditions of the global economy. I shall portray it in terms of a number of fractures or fault lines that divide aspects of academics' lives which they struggle to bring into more productive relationships through argument and debate. The tension between contestation and compliance, which is a major theme of this book, is particularly marked along these fault lines. They exist, and are widening, between teachers and students, between teaching and management, between teaching and research, and between the increasingly fragmented areas of knowledge, and no doubt between other aspects of our academic practice. I will suggest that the function often called 'Academic Development' must concern itself with the process of re-integration in the face of these disintegrating or fragmenting pressures. By 're-integration', rather than 'reintegration', I mean a search for new forms of integrity in the face of the complexity of present circumstances.

We saw in Chapter 3 how some Russian academics regretted the loss of a sense of solidarity amongst their students as the old communistic structures of society were removed. But they did not want to return to those structures. Or the South African lecturers who could no longer view the democratization of the classroom within the framework of an integrated opposition to the earlier apartheid regime, but would not wish to return to those days. Similarly, in the university community generally, I am not going to argue for a return to the traditional and relatively stable relationships between teachers and learners, academics and their leaders, or between disciplines, that is characteristic of an elite system of higher education. It is not a question of returning to some imagined golden age of academic coherence within securely bounded disciplines. Rather the task of academic development will be to attempt to reassert and reinterpret academic values into a professional experience that is becoming increasingly incoherent as it attempts to serve a wider and often conflicting range of social purposes and a wider cross-section of society.

These fault lines are critical. By this I mean that each raises important questions about what it is to be an academic. They indicate that the very idea of academic practice, or of the academic as a professional, even the word 'academic' itself, is contested. Indeed, academic work at institutions of higher education is conducted by people occupying various roles, including researchers, learning technologists, academic developers, multimedia specialists and learning managers. At the same time, many universities have a grouping termed 'Academic Committee' which, in some institutions, concerns itself with the university's policies and practices in general, in others mainly with research and gaining research income, and in yet others is concerned only with teaching.

In the face of the consequent uncertainties about roles and relationships, there is a need to articulate what is meant by academic work appropriate to this changed context. If it is to be academic (or scholarly), rather than merely technical, then those who occupy academic roles need to engage with this contestation about work and roles and struggle to create, or at least shape, their identities, rather than be shaped solely by external forces. I suggested in the last chapter that teachers, in various levels of educational institutions, have attempted to reinterpret external imperatives associated with the skills agenda. In relation to the fragmented experience along the various fault lines in higher education, university staff need to struggle to reinterpret other imposed requirements.

The process of academic development therefore involves professional development. Unless academics can exert at least some control over the nature of their work, and give some sense of coherence to it, it cannot really be considered to be professional.

If academic development is to be a re-integrating force in academic life, then how it does so will depend upon how the wider social purposes of academic life are understood. How it shapes new relationships between fragmented aspects of academic work depends upon its vision of the purposes of higher education.

But as soon as we talk of 'educational purposes' the first fault line suggests itself: the tension between how students, their teachers and the external stakeholders view the purpose of higher education.

Fault line 1: the purposes of higher education

The pre-university student whose comment opened the first chapter wanted to go to university to make the world a better place; while politicians, with their concerns for how universities are to be funded, invariably speak as though universities serve purely economic interests. Vice Chancellors speak of 'internationalizing' the curriculum in order to position their institutions in the global market; while organizations and associations concerned with global citizenship (such as the Development Education Association, in the UK) understand 'internationalization' and the future role of higher education in terms of addressing the inequalities and poor social conditions amongst many of the world's populations. The lecturers in Chapter 3 talked about the critical purposes of university teaching; while their students, so they claimed, tended to have very instrumental ideas about higher education, usually in terms of getting jobs.

But such generalizations and stereotypes can be misleading. When the UK Secretary of State for Education was accused in the press of valuing higher education only in terms of employment, he claimed he had been misunderstood (Clarke 2003). The Russian students reported in Chapter 3 demonstrated a high degree of sensitivity to suffering in the wider world, even though their lecturers had claimed that they were disinterested in political and social affairs.

When those lecturers viewed their students as being instrumental in their values, perhaps they were projecting onto their students their own feelings of frustration and cynicism, due to the pressures under which they worked. They may have been inclined to blame their students instead of the social circumstances that have shaped their values. While any such interpretation is highly speculative, what was striking was the extent to which the lecturers identified *their* purposes as higher educators to be in sharp contrast with what they thought *their students* perceived to be the purpose of their study. Their students' views, so they claimed, reflected the views of the wider society, whereas the lecturers were more inclined to see their purpose in terms of such aims as developing 'critique', 'social transformation' and 'questioning attitude'. It is, perhaps, a commonplace for lecturers to contrast their students' instrumental and 'surface' (or 'strategic') learning with their own.

This immediately raises an interesting area for enquiry. Are higher education teachers making assumptions about their students' purposes? Are students making assumptions about lecturers'? How valid are such assumptions? A lot of attention has been given to teaching methods that might encourage 'surface' rather than 'deep' learning (since Marton *et al.* 1993, 1997). The literature in the broad field of teaching and learning in higher education, however, is remarkably silent about the purposes of the learning that it claims to promote (Malcolm and Zukas 2001). Without an understanding of its purpose, concepts about the depth of learning are meaningless. A railway manager may need to have a deep understanding of a timetable, while my own understanding, as a passenger, needs only to be superficial. The depth of learning that is appropriate depends upon the purpose to which it is put. Teachers are required by quality assurance regimes to specify the aims and objectives of their teaching. But again, the wider purposes go largely unexamined.

The same argument can, and should, be developed in relation to research. Raising research capacity, which is a concern of research funding councils, pays scant regard to raising awareness and consciousness of the different, and at times competing, kinds of social values and interests that research may contribute to society at large. A research community that engages with society is one that is aware of its responsibilities, not simply one that is concerned to raise capacity and output regardless of consequences. And part of that responsibility consists in engaging in the wider debate about how research in their field might contribute to society.

If, as it appears, there is a tension between university teachers' and their students' perceptions about each other's purposes, then it needs to be understood. One of the few things that cognitive scientists agree about is that a clear sense of purpose is important for successful learning. Students and teachers may both have suffered from the distorting influences of the global economy, commercialism, centralized control and so on, which have narrowed their vision of higher education. But both groups need to join together in attempting to understand each other's perceptions about this. It is taken for granted that the aim of teaching is for the learner and teacher to share some understanding regarding the subject matter to be taught. It is less readily assumed that they should share an understanding regarding the purposes to which such knowledge might be put.

I am not suggesting that learners should understand what they are taught in the same way as their lecturers: 'sharing an understanding' is not the same as 'having the same understanding'. To do so would presuppose a transmissive model of teaching and be opposed to a constructive model of learning which underlies an enquiry approach. Equally, I am not suggesting that lecturers and their students should share the *same* purposes when they set about the educational enterprise in general. But just as teaching and learning should involve a serious attempt by the teacher and learner to understand each other's understanding of what is being taught, so they should attempt to understand each other's understanding about why it should be learnt.

The same relationship holds in respect of researchers and the bodies who fund research. A member of a team researching a new pharmaceutical product may be driven by curiosity and the pursuit of knowledge for its own sake; or be motivated by a concern to achieve well in the next research assessment. Such interests may be very different from those of the funding commercial organization that may stand to make financial gains from its outcomes. But for the researchers to make no attempt to understand the wider social and economic purposes of their research, and of those who provide its funding, would be irresponsible. Justifiable claims have been made that academic freedom has been undermined by research funding arrangements (for example, by Evans 2002), but at least some of the responsibility for this may, on occasion, lie with academic staff and their managers who may not have enquired too deeply into the purposes to which their research may be put or the commercial context in which it was funded.

A concern of academic development, I suggest, should be to raise the debate about the purpose of higher education. This debate must be taken up amongst those involved in academic work and directed towards policy makers. It should not only be conducted in places removed from students and researchers, however, but also should be contested and negotiated with them. Lecturers' purposes, and their students', may not always be reconcilable. Nor may the views of researchers and their funders. But they should be articulated. Neither academics nor students should acquiesce in the assumption that education is merely instrumental. Curiosity and the excitement of discovery may not figure high on the motivations of Ministers of State for Higher Education, but they are not yet totally eradicated from the experience of students, their teachers or researchers.

Raising such a question about the views of students, and how we might negotiate such a difficult question with them, requires a particular way of conceiving of the relationships between teacher, learner and subject matter, which will be explored in Chapter 8. It also involves a culture of communication between students and teachers. But this culture of communication has also become fragmented, indicating a second fault line that academic development needs to address.

Fault line 2: between teachers and students

Communication between teachers and learners is naturally of major interest to anyone who teaches or thinks about teaching. The relationships between student and teacher, and therefore the forms of communication between them, have for some time been changing towards a model in which the student is cast as customer or client and the teacher as service deliverer (see, for example, how Levacic 1993 is reported in Warhurst 2001: 84–5).

As an aspect of this, consider the ways in which students evaluate their learning experience. Standardized evaluation forms are now commonplace. Modelled on customer satisfaction surveys, it has been suggested (Johnson 2000) that students often view such feedback with cynicism, that it can undermine communicative relationships between teachers and learners, and that rather than empowering students it serves the bureaucratic function of controlling both teachers and students. Inasmuch as the student is indeed empowered as a client, it is a form of empowerment that is likely to lead to an increasingly litigious relationship as students resort to legal means to address their grievances and frustrations in the face of an inadequately resourced higher education. This is very different from empowerment that is based on trust, which is essential for learners and teachers to enquire collaboratively.

This presents an interesting challenge to academic development. Granted that teachers should be accountable to their students for their teaching, how can this be done in ways that enhance, rather than undermine, the communicative relationships between teachers and students? How can students be engaged with their teachers in evaluating their experience of being taught, rather than merely subjected to satisfaction measures? In fact many teachers in all disciplines hold discussions or tutorials in which their students are encouraged to reflect upon and evaluate the teaching they receive. The status of such evaluation, being qualitative and formative, however, is invariably undervalued or ignored by quality assurance procedures which are principally concerned with quantitative and summative measures. What is required here is an approach that is much closer to the principles of action research, which seeks to enhance the students' experience through the very process of enquiring into it.

It is a challenge for academic development to devise such procedures and influence the quality assurance policies in which they are enmeshed. Quality managers need to be helped to understand the limitations of reductive measures and shown how qualitative and reflective accounts of practice might be more useful.

But viewing the problem this way immediately confronts us with another fault line: that between the teachers who inevitably are responsible for the quality of their teaching and the managers who determine the means by which it, and the consequent learning, is to be assured.

Fault line 3: between teachers and managers

Bureaucratic forms of accountability have not only led to a widening gap between teachers and their students, but also between teachers and their managers. An older style of 'command structure' (Charlton 1999) in which a manager, such as a head of department, may have required a lecturer to give an account of his or her teaching, was at least a relationship of power which was transparent, immediate and, in a sense, intimate. It was, in principle, open to negotiation. Now this has been replaced by a remote system of control in which external standards and quality assurance procedures are handed down. In the UK (where centralized control is more predominant than, for example, in the USA where market forces have a greater impact), academic staff wait with bated breath for the rules of the next assessment or review to be made of teaching or research.

In this climate, managers and administrators are likely to be viewed by academic staff as being part of a culture of compliance and as agents of the external forces whose values they reject. Their influence is increasingly viewed with suspicion by academic staff. The academic development work of those in centralized staff and educational development units is often led by such external agendas as employability, diversity or transferable skills. In these cases, it can also become associated with the culture of compliance in the eyes of academic staff in disciplinary departments.

This was the case when I arrived at my present post as a professor of higher education in a research-led university. In this case, it led to a somewhat ironic situation. On first meeting the head of a very successful disciplinary department, I was told that my own unit – a central unit which is primarily concerned with research and development into teaching and learning in the university – will only succeed if it distances itself from the culture of compliance. My unit should have nothing to do with the institutionalized forms of quality assurance regimes, he said. I was inclined to agree. Setting aside such bureaucratic concerns, we had an interesting and in-depth discussion about his field and the relationships between teaching and research in his department. This soon led us to planning a collaborative research project on the matter.

Imagine my surprise when, a few days later, I received a message from him saying that our project to explore the relationship between teaching and research would look good, and he would make sure it was noted, in both his department's teaching quality and research assessment documentation. The irony did not escape either of us. On this occasion, driven by an academic interest, we could, somewhat paradoxically, advance the instrumental interests of quality assurance. This was a clear instance of the kind of innovation, suggested in the last chapter in relation to the skills agenda, in which critical compliance is possible. While external imposition may at times be something to struggle against, at others it is important to search for those opportunities that serve the interests of both external requirements and academic development. Even contradictory forces can sometimes, at a local level, be brought into some degree of alignment.

Normally, however, academic and managerial priorities cannot so easily be aligned. In these cases there should be no doubt about where the interests of academic development lie. Academic development involves the development and promotion of academic values, if necessary resisting any bureaucratic imperatives that compromise it. Thus, while working in the fracture between academic and managing staff, the emphasis should be upon reminding management of its academic values, rather than reminding academics of their managerial responsibilities.

The fracturing of higher education goes much deeper, however, than the relationships and value differences between those who occupy different roles. It shapes the very language we use about higher education and the practice that is managed. In particular, academic practice has come to be conceptualized largely in terms of two separate activities, teaching and research. It is this relationship that presents us with the next critical fault line.

Fault line 4: between teaching and research

There is a controversial debate about how teaching and disciplinary research are related. There are those who view the close relationships between teaching and research as a myth to be challenged, and others who see both activities as being fundamental aspects of the academic's work and the university's purpose. The terms of this debate, and the emerging publications, however, are predominantly conceptualized around such functional questions as whether or not good teachers are also good researchers (Hattie and Marsh 1996; Qamar uz Zaman 2004), or whether or not an emphasis on one of these aspects supports, or detracts from, an emphasis upon the other. While the conclusions of such studies vary widely, their functionalist assumptions about the nature of each serve only to reinforce the separation between them. Boyer (1990) identified four different types of scholarship which include disciplinary research (the scholarship of discovery) and the scholarship of teaching. While his descriptions have some subtlety, and he was certainly in favour of drawing closer relationships between teaching and research, any such categorization is liable to drive a wedge between the two once such categories form the basis of funding arrangements. In this respect it is useful to bear in mind Bourdieu's observation that the categories of teaching and research 'prevent us from conceptualizing the university field' because they fail to recognize its complexity (Bourdieu 1988: 13). This was also a clear finding of an empirical enquiry in a UK university (see Rowland 1996).

Such poor conceptualization undermined a fundamental review of the UK Research Assessment Exercise (RAE) that was conducted by HEFCE in 2000. This acknowledged that the financial rewards, which have been directed towards successful research output, have had a negative impact upon teaching. In recommending how future funding for research should be directed, however, the report stated that it would be wrong to alter present arrangements for this reason. Instead, 'it is necessary to create other and parallel reward systems so that academic staff and their institutions see incentives to put their effort into activities other than research, in which they might have greater strengths or can add more value' (HEFCE 2000: 20).

Here we can see how the perception of teaching and research as separate functions, driven by separate reward structures, undermines the coherence of academic practice. It is by such means that successive RAEs have led to 'a gradual separation, structurally, of research and teaching' (McNay 1998: 196). This fragmenting influence was exacerbated by the UK government's White Paper *The Future of Higher Education* (DfES 2003), which sought to separate funding for teaching and research further and concentrate research excellence in a few universities.

A more integrative policy would, for example, be more concerned to reward research into teaching in the disciplines, or reward disciplinary research that has a more immediate impact upon teaching, or reward teaching that involves methods that stimulate research. In the USA, for example, the National Science Foundation is particularly concerned to reward scientific research that can be used to enhance teaching. All of these are possible. But instead *The Future of Higher Education*, and the plans for the subsequent assessment exercise of 2008, miss the opportunity through a narrowly functionalist approach: academic practice is reduced to discrete, separate and almost unrelated functions.

Such policies and funding decisions serve to emphasize the differences rather than the similarities between teaching and research. As a consequence, academic staff experience even greater tensions between requirements to succeed in terms of research measures and teaching measures.

In the UK, the Institute for Learning and Teaching in Higher Education (ILTHE) was set up in 1999 with the specific objective of enhancing the status of teaching. In 2005 this was incorporated into the Higher Education Academy (HEA), whose mission was to help institutions 'to provide for the best possible learning experience for their students' (HEA 2005: 4). While ILTHE and HEA have both, to varying degrees, been concerned to support pedagogical research, or research into teaching and learning, neither has viewed disciplinary research as being a part of academic practice which they are concerned to enhance. Thus there is a danger that, far from providing some counterbalance to the high status accorded to research, they will serve merely to emphasize the separation between teaching and research that was underlined by the White Paper (DfES 2003).

In addressing the fault line between teaching and research, academic development requires a more fundamental debate about the relationships between the two. As a start, this debate should help us to reconceptualize such terms as 'research-led teaching', 'the discipline' and 'scholarship', which frequently turn up in documentation about teaching and learning, often with little understanding of what they mean. Here we can see how academic development might be understood in terms of the academic community's attempt to reappropriate the language by which academic practice is articulated. Such a task would help us to deconstruct terms like 'delivery', 'objectives', 'good practice', 'excellence' and 'skill', which form the reductive discourse that undermines our ability to articulate academic practice. It is a task that should not be confined to educationists. It can emerge naturally enough when academics from different disciplines are given the space and encouragement to speak to each other about their work in terms that matter to them (see, for example, Jenkins 1996 or Rowland 2000). It is out of such real academic engagement that the narrative of higher education needs to be written, rather than from the managerialist discourse that views higher education as an industry whose outcomes must be controlled and assured.

This emphasis upon the differences between teaching and research arises from a view of research as the creation of knowledge, narrowly reified as a commodity. Policy documents on research typically emphasize how research is needed to fill 'gaps in knowledge' (NERF 2000: 6) rather than offer new interpretations; to discover how to do things rather than question why such things should be done; to find out how best to execute policies rather than develop critiques of them.

Such commodification of knowledge leads inevitably to an apparent increase in the quantity of knowledge and consequently to fragmentation. It becomes increasingly impossible for anyone to be familiar with more than a small fragment of the total. This represents my final fault line.

Fault line 5: the fragmentation of knowledge

In Chapter 2 I indicated how the rapid expansion of knowledge and specialization had led to the emergence of many new sub-disciplines over the last 20 years. If 8500 different specialities in the sciences were identified during the 1990s (Clark 2000), then it is hardly surprising that academics often feel they share few intellectual interests even with others in their own department, let alone those in other discipline areas. Moreover, as disciplines become increasingly broken down into more highly specialized sub-disciplines, so the very idea of the discipline itself becomes redundant. Indeed, there are those who argue that the very concept of the discipline is no longer meaningful. We might view this breakdown as part of what postmodernists would call the death of theory.

These radical changes in the disciplines can lead to creative opportunities for critical interdisciplinarity, as I suggested in Chapter 2 and will develop further in Chapter 7. In practice, however, this fragmentation often amounts to a closing down amongst academics of opportunities for critical debate informed by their scholarly work. As experts in their own field, they are rarely challenged to use that expertise to engage critically with the wider purposes of their work. The scientist working in one of 8500 specialities is unlikely to ask questions about the purpose of science as a whole. Opportunities for meeting colleagues from different disciplines invariably revolve around mundane practical or managerial matters. At such meetings, teaching is often viewed as being practical and managerial since it is described in terms of the reductive language of managerialism.

This presents a fundamental challenge to academic development. Those with a primary role to promote academic development have typically seen this as a generic, practical and instrumental activity largely divorced from the serious intellectual work of research. An opportunity is lost. For the development of teaching could provide the opportunity for critical engagement between disciplines. When academics are given the opportunity to talk about learning in their disciplines in a way that goes beyond the instrumental approach of quality assurance, they begin to experience how the very concepts they use are rooted in different disciplinary frameworks. In this way conversation about teaching and the curriculum can provide the very key to enabling critical debate between academics from different disciplines, rather than a mundane matter far removed from their disciplinary interests.

Here is a very simple example (Rowland 2000: 58). A cell biologist and a systems engineer were talking about feedback. For the systems engineer feedback is a mechanism for controlling a mechanical system so that it performs in the same predictable way. For a cell biologist it is a means whereby an organic system (a cell) can develop in response to its changing environment. How then are we to understand feedback as teachers? Is the appropriate metaphor one of mechanical control or organic development? It is easy to see how quality assurance ways of thinking on this matter are informed by a mechanical, controlling metaphor, rather than an organic, developmental one. The very languages that different disciplines can bring to bear upon issues of teaching and learning can challenge and deepen both disciplinary thinking and educational ideas.

It follows that the development of teaching and learning in higher education is best not seen simply in terms of questions about how to teach. If it is, it will readily be sucked into the reductive discourse of the culture of compliance. On the contrary, it provides an opportunity to bring the different disciplines into a critical relationship as they each explore the nature of the knowledge with which they deal. In this way, efforts to develop teaching across disciplinary boundaries can directly help to overcome the fragmentation of the disciplines through debate and contestation. They can also help develop interdisciplinarities which are challenging and critical.

Curriculum discussion that raises awareness of the nature of the disciplines also helps keep them alive. A head of an architecture department to whom I spoke attempted to explain to me the nature of his discipline. 'Architecture,' he said, 'is a discipline in which the question "what is architecture?" must always be a valid and live question. Once we stop asking that question, the discipline is dead' (Rowland 2002a). We might say the same for any discipline: it must always be based upon contestation. While debate about the nature of the discipline may come more naturally within the arts and humanities, it is increasingly important within the sciences as new disciplines emerge. Such contestation can readily take place on the interfaces between disciplines. It enhances the intellectual rigour of research and the integrity of teaching, both of which are undermined by the reductive discourses of the culture of compliance. Within our fragmented culture, such interaction too rarely takes place. Academic development involves creating spaces for such contestation.

Conclusion

I have argued that the fragmented nature of higher education is experienced in terms of a number of fractures or fault lines. I have chosen to concentrate here on five: the diverse assumptions about the nature of higher education; the separation between teachers and learners; the separation between academic staff and those who manage them; the split between teaching and research; and the fragmented nature of knowledge itself. One could identify other areas in which fragmentation manifests itself: between research and policy; between theory and practice; or, at a more philosophical level, between matters of fact and value. Policy initiatives have tended to aggravate rather than ameliorate these fractures. I suggest that an aim of academic development is to create coherence in academic practice by working within these fractures. To achieve this, there needs to be a series of critical conversations between teachers and learners, between academics and managers and between the disciplines. Such conversations might be seen as contributing to the development of a new academic professionalism (Nixon *et al.* 2001) as academic workers struggle to form new relationships across the fault lines of their fragmented world. This is characterized by an 'intellectual sociability' (p. 241) in which academics, students and the wider community think together for the common good, whilst recognizing difference and diversity. The first and foremost subject of this thinking together must concern the purposes of higher education itself.

Academic development takes place largely in the spaces created by fragmentation in higher education. But what is the nature of such work? Whose task is it to do this, and how does it relate to the more established academic activities of teaching and research? These are the questions to which I now want to turn.

6

Academic development

A site of contestation

A senior manager described his university as aiming to become a 'truly global' UK institution. He was asked in the press to comment on the research function of a unit which had been recently reorganized to support academic departments towards this aim. He said: 'We are not saying the unit cannot do research, but it has to be on issues of direct importance to [the institution], which is very different from the blue skies research that members of an academic department would expect to undertake' (Lipsett 2004).

Academic development is intertwined with the micro politics of the institution as well as the wider politics of higher education. It is an aspect of academic work that demands courage in the face of pressures to conform from within and beyond the university. If an important concern of academic development is to meet the educational needs of students, and also of the wider society that benefits from the teaching and research of universities, who is to decide upon those needs? And where do educational values fit into this?

In the light of the comments of the senior manager, further questions follow. What kind of research is involved in academic development? How is it similar to and different from research in other areas, and why? In what sense is it (or is it not) academic? Who decides what is of importance to the institution? What limits do such decisions impose upon academic development research? Can such research reflect critically upon the institution's policies or is it merely an instrument of management? What are the implications of this for 'academic freedom'?

These kinds of questions need to be addressed if the university is to develop itself by reflecting critically upon its practice. They indicate the position of academic development at the heart of the tension between compliance and contestation. They are therefore of fundamental importance to the enquiring university. In attempting to answer them, I hope to indicate the nature of academic development work and the identities of academic developers.

My attempt to untangle such questions will lead to the conclusion that universities need to create more appropriate spaces within which to reflect upon their development. This might involve giving much more serious attention to the field of higher education studies as providing an academic context for academic development. It might also lead institutions to set up departments of higher education studies.

Academic development as critical engagement

Some provisional definitions are needed for the central terms of this discussion: 'teaching', 'learning', 'academic practice' and 'academic development'. In the last chapter I suggested that one consequence of the fragmented nature of higher education is that the meanings of many of the central terms that describe university work have become contested and fluid. This is, of course, part of the difficulty faced when any attempt is made to redefine the purposes, or retell the story, of higher education. The definitions I offer are therefore provisional and restricted to the purposes of this discussion.

Teaching describes what people typically do when working directly or indirectly with students with the intention of guiding their learning. Learning describes what students and lecturers sometimes, but not always, achieve as a consequence of being taught. The distinction between teaching as something that is done and learning as something that is achieved is significant.

Learning also describes an important consequence that may arise from doing research, both for researchers and for those to whom their research is disseminated. There are also, of course, many other things that may lead to learning, which are not of central concern here.

Academic practice includes research as well as teaching, and the learning that results from both. It also includes the other activities that are essential to being part of an academic community in which individuals aim to learn and encourage the learning of others.

Academic development is then the development of such academic practice. It depends upon learning about academic practice: learning, that is, about the nature of learning, teaching and research. It also depends upon putting this learning about academic practice into effect. It is therefore a theoretical and practical activity. Its theoretical and practical aspects are so closely intertwined that it is sometimes unhelpful to attempt to distinguish the two. This intertwining of theory and practice in academic development has close links with Aristotle's conception of *praxis* and also, in a rather different way, with the currently fashionable term 'reflective practice'.

Since learning, research and teaching take place within a collegial community, academic development is also a social process. Research in the field is therefore informed by sociological understandings.

Central to the practice and theory of academic development must be an engagement between those who are to learn about their academic practices in order to develop them. This engagement is academic in two different ways. First, it involves learning and so is an academic process. Second, its subject matter concerns academic practice. Academic development is thus a doubly academic practice: it is an academic practice about academic practices. In this respect it is different from most academic activity that takes place in academic departments. It is reflexive in the strong sense that a major aspect of its subject matter is its process of enquiry.

In the light of the previous chapter's discussion, one consequence of the ways in which academic life is fragmented is that academic development work, which is doubly academic, is also fragmented at two levels. Its subject matter (that is, the academic practices within the university generally) is fragmented and its academic pursuit (that is, the development of these practices) is also fragmented. It is thus not surprising that empirical studies in the UK and Australasia have shown it to be 'a fragmented community of practice' (Land 2001: 4) and one whose participants have 'divergent' and 'contradictory conceptions of their profession' (Fraser 2001: 54).

Furthermore, those who identify themselves with the academic development community (including educational developers, academic staff developers, instructional developers, faculty developers) might be expected to have a particular difficulty when it comes to articulating their own identity. That this appears to be the case is illustrated by the fact that, out of 45 articles in three consecutive volumes (2001–04) of the *International Journal of Academic Development*, a leading journal for academic developers, no less than 15 focused upon the role and identity of academic (or educational) developers. It would appear from this that those who conduct research in the field of academic development spend a third of their time wondering who they are.

A characteristic feature of an academic practice is that it is critical. Teachers in higher education aim for their students to be critical, to think critically, or engage critically with the subject matter of their studies. What is meant by 'critical' in this context varies widely. For some it is a propensity for 'deep' (as opposed to 'surface') learning (as in, for example, Marton *et al.* 1993, 1997). Others focus on critical thought, and critical thinking (e.g. Browne and Freeman 2000). For others the idea is that students should develop powers of critical self-reflection and critical action (Barnett 1997).

Whatever view is taken about this, however, inasmuch as academics expect a critical engagement on the part of their students, one must expect no less of them as they struggle to understand their own professional practices. If higher education is a critical business for students, so must it be for those who teach them and conduct research.

It is claimed (for example by Bath and Smith 2004: 14) that academic developers have a particular responsibility to be critical in their practice. Such a view might seem to be supported by my claim that academic development is doubly academic. It may be arrogant, however, to suppose that academic developers possess any particular critical faculties compared to their colleagues. But more importantly, an enquiring university presupposes that all those involved in its educational work do so with a spirit of critical enquiry. I suggested in the last chapter that academic developers should be involved in 'reminding management of its academic values, rather than reminding academics of their managerial responsibilities' (p. 68). But this is not to say that academic developers are the sole guardians of academic values, of which criticality is one.

How, then, are academics to develop critical ways of engaging with one another? This presents our first problem. How can they speak to each other, and learn from each other, across the divided fault lines between the disciplines and roles which they take on? At a practical level, what and how can a dentist learn from a historian about teaching, learning or research? At a more theoretical or philosophical level, what assumptions about what it means to know something underlie dentistry and history and how do they differ? What are the implications of these differences upon how they teach, learn and conduct their research?

I shall address these questions here primarily, though not exclusively, in relation to the development of teaching. The next chapter will address some similar questions more specifically in relation to research. For those concerned to develop teaching in higher education, the challenge is to join with academics in a discourse of learning that is critical in a context that is fragmented. I now want to consider the nature of this engagement.

Generic approaches

Academic staff come from backgrounds with very different traditions of thought, and ways of expressing their ideas and interests. If they are to speak together about questions of learning it would be convenient to view such matters as largely generalizable across disciplines. This is the common assumption: that although university teachers are scholars of a particular subject, questions about the development of learning, and thus academic development generally, are of a different order. From this viewpoint, the academic dentist and the historian have much to learn about the nature of learning (and how to do it and support it) which is independent of their subject. Starting from this premise, one of two different conclusions is often drawn: one emphasizes the practical, craft aspect of teaching; the other emphasizes its theoretical roots.

According to this first *atheoretical approach*, teaching and learning and their development are primarily practical, rather than theoretical, activities. Teaching is a set of crafts or skills and interventions that can be learnt through familiarity. It may require effort, but the nature of this effort is not primarily intellectual. According to this view, the academic's intellectual efforts should be directed primarily towards research. This is not necessarily to downgrade the task of teaching, its difficulties or the rewards it provides. These rewards are seen in terms such as the satisfaction of seeing students grasp new ideas, celebrating their achievements, fulfilling one's duty towards them, providing a stimulating environment and so on. Such values are vital to a higher education community. They should indeed be as much a part of the value system that underlies research as one that underlies teaching. Such a view of teaching dichotomizes teaching and research. Teaching is seen in terms of practice and skill, research in terms of theory and knowledge. In the last chapter I showed the limitations of this view for research training. The same limitations apply to teaching in general.

This *atheoretical approach* to teaching and its development contrasts with the idea of an enquiring university in which teaching and research are both based upon intellectual enquiry which has both theoretical and practical aspects. A consequence of the *atheoretical approach* is that the development of university teaching is largely a matter of academics taking part in programmes of training to ensure they gain the necessary familiarity and practice and absorb the appropriate values.

The job of the academic development worker, according to this view of teaching, is to provide training in the craft of teaching. Such a role is not theoretically based. In a university culture which traditionally values its intellectual contribution to society, it is not surprising that, from this atheoretical perspective, teaching is viewed as a somewhat menial and amateurish task compared to the real intellectual work of research (Booth 1998: 1), and those concerned to develop it are trainers rather than educators. Where such training for university staff is provided by development workers whose job status is not academic, this perception of the role of teaching is likely to be reinforced.

A different conclusion, which could be drawn from the assumption that teaching is largely generalizable across different subject matters, is that teaching is more than a practical craft but is theoretically based. Its theoretical basis is to be found within the study of education. Academic developers, from this perspective, are educationalists rather than trainers, and questions about teaching and learning and their development are the special concern of their educational research. This research aims to develop educational theory, albeit educational theory related specifically to the phase of higher education.

According to this *educational approach*, the development of an academic's teaching is a consequence of his or her introduction to a specifically educational way of thinking. It might be unrealistic, however, to expect an academic who is a historian or dentist also to be an educationalist, for the study of education is a different discipline with its own characteristics. It follows from this that the development of university teaching should be guided by academic developers who theorize, conduct research and produce 'findings' about teaching and learning. These findings would then be applied by the non-educationalist academics in their discipline. It is an activity that, although directed towards the development of academic practices, is theoretically based. The theories involved are educational theories.

Following recent initiatives in many countries (especially Australia, the UK and New Zealand) that have been aimed at raising the status of teaching, academic developers have increasingly been appointed on academic (rather than academic-related or administrative) grades, up to the level of professor. This would appear to reflect a growing trend towards viewing them as researchers and experts in education, whose activity is more academic and who have a more theoretical understanding.

Furthermore, Bath and Smith (2004: 12) note 14 internationally recognized journals in the field, claiming this as evidence that the field has become more securely established as a disciplinary tribe. This may also have increased the credibility of academic developers in the eyes of their colleagues in the disciplines.

The extent to which academic developers in fact have a background in education is, however, limited. In Australasia, which is probably further along this path than the UK, a study in 1999 showed that 63 per cent of academic developers had a teaching qualification, with 50 per cent at Masters level (Fraser 1999). These figures have no doubt risen considerably since then. But the proportion of academic developers with a PhD in education, academic development or higher education is a very small minority. On these grounds alone, if academic development constitutes a theoretically based field of study, it is not at all clear that education, as a discipline, is a necessary constituent of it.

Critical interdisciplinarity

I am somewhat sceptical, however, of both the atheoretical and the educational models of academic development. I would question the premise upon which both are based: that teaching and learning are largely generic. Such a view is inclined to lead to an undue emphasis on the applied psychology of learning.

While learning how to fill a tooth, or interpret a historical text, or investigate sub-atomic particles might have some interesting things in common, the differences between them might be even more revealing. As historians and dentists explore ways of developing their teaching and learning, they are likely to think differently by virtue of their different academic backgrounds. These differences will shape the ways they think about their teaching and learning.

Valuing the insights, concerns and epistemological assumptions that are particular to the different disciplines, Jenkins (1996) argued that an effective context for academic development is with colleagues working in mixed groups but from their disciplinary perspectives. He goes on to suggest that 'even with workshops drawing on staff from a range of disciplines, it may be appropriate initially to centre the course on disciplinary concerns ... but to do so at a meta-level' (pp. 54–5). But why is this only an 'initial' part of the process?

Like the staff at Stanford University, to whom Jenkins refers here, the experience of working with mixed groups of lecturers at Sheffield University, UK (Rowland 2000) suggested that they learn much from each other by drawing upon these differences, rather than by submerging them within the generic aspects of teaching. But more than this, such encounters in a mixed setting provide an opportunity for these disciplinary epistemologies, assumptions, concerns, or just plain customary practices to be challenged by others from different backgrounds.

This perspective is interdisciplinary. It is at the point of such challenges that critique can emerge. A historian, for example, is likely to have a different understanding of the status of data and its interpretation than a dentist. This will influence how they evaluate the nature of evidence within their own disciplines and also their assumptions about the evidence they might use in making judgements about their teaching. In such a climate of critique, academic development can become an interdisciplinary field that is critical. *Critical interdisciplinarity* involves the learner (as student, teacher or researcher) in confronting the critique that emerges as different disciplines contest each other's theoretical frameworks, perspectives and practices.

Adopting the perspective of academic development that is critical in this sense suggests a different model for teacher development than either the atheoretical generic perspective or the educational generic perspective. It might therefore be useful to summarize how these different emphases might influence the aims of courses in the development of teaching. It goes without saying that these three perspectives are not mutually exclusive, nor do they indicate rigid boundaries. No doubt any academic developer will recognize some of each in their own practice. But they do constitute different approaches to the field of teacher development.

Academic development courses

The *atheoretical approach* will give priority to methods for solving the practical problems of teaching: how to encourage 'deep' as opposed to 'surface' approaches to learning; how teachers can encourage students to become more involved; how to give effective lectures and run seminars and tutorials. Such matters are not simple or straightforward, but their focus is on the practical. The questions they address are principally in the form of 'how?', in which the experience of others will be important in order to draw upon a wide resource of practical ideas and strategies. The outcomes of courses adopting such an approach would be expressed in terms of competent and skilful practice on the part of participating teachers.

The *educational approach* is also concerned to improve practice, but this is seen to be based upon understanding educational theories. The questions it addresses will be principally of the form 'why?' In answering such questions recourse will be made to different educational theories. Distinctions between 'deep' and 'surface' learning, for example, would not be taken at face value. The concepts would be questioned in terms of their educational basis. The aim of courses adopting such an approach would be to enhance the ability to make educational judgements. Competent and skilful practice, from this perspective, will be seen to arise from the application of educational judgement that the course will seek to develop. The ability to make such judgements from theoretical knowledge will enable participants to respond critically to new ideas and developments in teaching.

The approach of *critical interdisciplinarity* would be of a different order from either of the above. Its theoretical basis would derive from the disciplinary perspectives of those involved. The differences underlying these perspectives would provide a basis for contestation between different and often conflicting views. Participants on such courses would not be expected to leave behind their disciplinary identity, but rather to sharpen that identity against the competing positions adopted by those from other disciplines. The question of 'deep' and 'surface' learning, for example, would not be a question of 'how to deliver it' or even 'why it is educationally significant' but rather, 'what does it amount to in the context of my discipline?'. A mathematician, for example, might argue that students need to know certain basic facts before they can go on to raise critical questions, even if only in a superficial manner. A sociologist, on the other hand, might claim that a critical or 'deep' approach to enquiry starts from the very earliest stages. These different assumptions might then inform the teaching methods adopted. While not all mathematicians or sociologists conform to such stereotypes of their disciplines, what is involved here is an encounter between different disciplinary epistemologies and cultures. In the process the mathematician and the sociologist might come to reflect upon some of their assumptions. The aim of a course to develop teaching from this perspective would be to widen the horizons of academic staff to different disciplinary perspectives in order to develop their understanding of the relationships between the forms of knowledge they teach and the methods that are consistent with them.

The debate that takes place on this kind of course, however, is not only about teaching but about the nature of the subject itself. Ideas about teaching methods which might arise from such discussion will be based upon a critical awareness of the disciplines involved and will therefore be closely related to questions of research methodology. For example, reflection upon the nature of evidence in a natural science and how this differs from evidence in a social science would inform the teaching content and the teaching processes and also be closely connected to the methodological concerns of researchers in their respective fields. Thus while the generic approaches tend to emphasize learning processes almost exclusively, a critical interdisciplinary approach draws attention to questions about the knowledge that is to be taught.

In this way, *critical interdisciplinarity* in development courses serves to draw teaching and research into closer relationships. They are viewed as different faces of enquiry with similar problems related to the subject matter, rather than as fundamentally different practices. The wider aim of development courses is no longer concerned with raising the status of teaching in relation to research but with supporting the intellectual integrity of enquiry. The aim for the historian on such a course, for example, is not only 'how shall I teach history?' but also 'what is it for my student (and indeed for me) to be a historian?' The idea of 'communities of practice' (Lave and Wenger 1999) into which students are increasingly drawn is an appropriate metaphor for such an approach.

Such questions are best addressed amongst participants from diverse disciplinary fields. Through debate with others they come to an awareness of their own presuppositions and are thereby able to subject them to scrutiny.

In terms of the discussion of fragmentation in the last chapter, such a course provides for an interesting space for academic development. It is a space that exists in the fractures between disciplines and sub-disciplines, but which can serve to have an integrative effect on the fracture between teaching and research. In the next chapter I shall explore further the nature of critical interdisciplinarity with more specific reference to research. In relation to the present discussion of teaching development, however, the aim of interdisciplinary contestation is not to merge or loosen disciplinary boundaries but rather to develop a clearer understanding of disciplinary difference and thus of disciplinarity as a dynamic and critical practice.

This does, however, leave the academic developer in an uncomfortable position. If not trainers in the craft of teaching, nor educationalists, what exactly are they? From the perspective of critical interdisciplinarity it seems that either too much or too little is expected of them. They could be viewed as skilful facilitators who draw academic staff together into a space where they explore their different approaches and learn from each other. But that seems to be a very limited role in which participants may do no more than defend and reinforce their own assumptions. Or they might be viewed as experts in all disciplines. As 'meta-disciplinarians', perhaps, they know enough to be able to draw upon the wide variety of expertise, forms of knowledge and disciplinary perspectives that might be encountered amongst the participants. They would be able to see how these might be deployed to develop different understandings about teaching.

This is surely too much to expect. Andresen, in a fictional dialogue in which an academic developer attempts to describe his work, suggests that academic developers are 'rather superior academics' (1996: 43). The expectation that academic developers might be masters of all trades, as well as adjudicators between the practitioners of trades, risks their becoming, in fact, masters of none, who lack credibility amongst all. These are real difficulties, but maybe ones that should be faced.

Settling the question of the disciplinary basis, or the particular form of expertise, that constitutes academic development work is a problem for academic developers. But I don't feel that they should be unduly anxious about being unable to resolve it. Universities typically have many departments that cannot readily be described in terms of one dominant discipline and are variously referred to as being multidisciplinary or interdisciplinary. Even within well-established disciplines, the nature of the discipline is often widely contested. And even where the discipline itself may not be so widely contested, a complex interplay between pure and applied subjects often renders the distinction obscure. In my own strongly research-led institution, the academic staff in the department of mathematics, for example, includes 13 professors whose research interests, in addition to pure mathematical aspects, include ecology, engineering, the environment and fluid mechanics as well as interdisciplinary research with psychologists, biologists and economists. Not many academic development units would span as wide a range of disciplines as that.

With such uncertainty and fluidity common across higher education, it would be wrong to believe that the status of academic developers depends upon theoretical security. The anxieties and insecurities of academic developers are real enough, but they are not principally a consequence of epistemological uncertainties and contestations around the nature of the field. On the contrary, contestation is an attribute of a healthy and dynamic field.

The question that needs to be addressed here is one of institutional power. Academic development suffers from a lack of positional power within the organization. This is needed if those involved in academic development are to be genuinely free to ask difficult questions and reveal uncomfortable truths. As presently organized they are largely constrained to conduct their enquiries within the parameters of institutional policies and priorities as these are defined by others.

The issue now becomes one of understanding the disciplinary basis of academic development in terms of its power base within the institution rather than its theoretical basis. If its task is really to stimulate critical debate, is it really free to do so? Who are the masters and who are the servants of academic development? Can academic developers contest their own institutions? And if they cannot, how can the institution enquire critically into its practice? These are the questions that I shall now address and propose the need for universities to embrace the field of higher education studies in order to gain a critical purchase on their development.

Academic development and higher education studies

A study by Gosling suggested that the senior management in institutions are unlikely to support courses or research in academic development that takes a critical stance (Gosling 1997: 214). My own experience was at odds with this (Rowland 2000: 39). HEIs are often complex and contradictory, valuing genuinely critical practice, while at the same time managing this in ways that minimize risk, maintain conformity and thereby inhibit critique. Since 2000, however, pressure has mounted for academic development to respond to external imperatives, with the danger of diminishing room for critical research into development. Academic development becomes more closely tied to the needs of the institution to meet external policy demands, towards which its stance is not expected to be critical.

In the UK, for example, one government policy, which became tied to 'formula funding', was to offer additional funds for teaching depending upon the institution's ability to attract students from a wider cross-section of society (HEFCE 2004: 2). The government had already set an objective for 50 per cent of 18- to 30-year-olds to participate in higher education by the end of 2009 (DfES 2003: Chapter 5).

In this situation one might expect an institution to be happy for its academic development unit to conduct research into widening access and participation and its implications for teaching. On the face of it, this would seem to be useful. But what if such research concluded that the institution should not pursue the government targets in this particular context? Such a research finding would probably be unacceptable since the implications of acting upon it would be a financial cost to the institution. In other words, the outcomes of academic development research are likely to be constrained by the institution's policy objectives which are, in turn, likely to be constrained by the national and institutional policy context.

This explains the senior manager's statement above that such research 'is very different from the blue skies research that members of an academic department would expect to undertake'. The issue at stake here is not about disciplinary competence, academic status or the frontiers of theoretical knowledge. Put quite simply, it is about the freedom to ask difficult questions and come to unpopular conclusions. It is a consequence of the lack of this freedom, rather than any theoretical basis, that academic developers' claims to be academic are limited. They are often denied the privilege of academic freedom by those who immediately fund their activity.

Academic freedom is essential to the very nature of academic work. Thus most countries have some Act or Regulation that stipulates that universities are required to protect academic freedom. In the UK, for example, the Education Reform Act 1988 requires universities to ensure that 'academic staff have freedom within the law to question and test received wisdom and to put forward new ideas and controversial or unpopular opinions' (DE 1988: Section 202(2)). Academic freedom is invariably one of the first casualties when democracy is threatened.

On this point, the tension between compliance and contestation is at its sharpest. Where (as is normally the case) academic development units are funded centrally by the university, it is understandable that their work, including their research, should be in support of institutional policies. Such research is often described as being 'institutional' and is contrasted with 'blue skies research that members of an academic department would expect to undertake' or, more simply, academic research.

If the research of academic developers in the field of higher education is to serve the needs of higher education as a whole, it must have the freedom of academic research to ask difficult questions as well as a focus that is relevant to institutions. A recent study indicates that outside the USA the capacity to undertake such higher education research that goes beyond 'undertaking research into institutional functioning as the need is perceived' is lacking (Yorke 2004: 141). Yorke argues that such capacity needs to be built up to ensure the continuing success of institutions and the sector as a whole.

Yorke argues that if universities limit their interest in higher education to research that is only in response to immediately perceived need, and limited by institutional policies, then this will only serve short-term interests. In other words, universities' longer-term interests are best served by researchers into higher education taking a critical perspective. Here the relationship between academic development and the university mirrors the relationship between higher education and the state. It should be one of critical, rather than compliant, service. In the longer term, society is not best served by universities simply doing as they are told without question. Similarly, universities will not be best served by academic developers whose service is merely compliant.

The location of academic development units in most institutions makes a critical, as opposed to compliant, approach difficult. They are normally organized as a subset of staff development, personnel or administration. Such units usually have a university-wide brief, although increasingly this brief is related to a particular faculty or school. They often contain academic developers who have an academic background in a discipline, a research record, and experience of teaching and research in higher education. They are often, indeed, the 'rather superior academics' of Andresen (1996: 43). But because their work in academic development is positioned within the organization as a support activity, it is not given academic credibility. While such lack of credibility has often been perceived in terms of a lack of academic rigour, my argument here is that the key limitation to this credibility consists in its lack of academic freedom and its dependence upon the immediate concerns of management. But how can centrally funded units be expected to have a degree of independence from the management to which they are accountable?

There could be two rather different kinds of independence sought here. One would be independence from those staff who hold the most senior management appointments in the institution, such as a senior management team. Another kind would be the independence from managerial, as opposed to academic, considerations.

To achieve independence from managerial considerations is particularly difficult when management itself is so diffused within the institution. Even in the most secure academic department, managerial and academic roles live uncomfortably side by side, and even intertwined. The fracture, identified in the last chapter, between managers and teachers is not so much a separation between two different groups of actual people, but rather a fracture between two different identities, cultures and discourses. In fact, many academic staff are often required to move between these two identities, with the consequent difficulty of maintaining personal integrity.

A degree of independence from senior managers, on the other hand, could be achieved if academic development units were repositioned as departments of higher education studies that are, in every sense, academic departments. The implications of this are that they would no longer be centrally funded directly. Their research funding would come from research councils and other external bodies, as in other disciplines. They would, however, also have a provider–client relationship with their host institutions. Rather like the close relationships that used to be very strong between university departments of education and local education authorities in the UK, such academic development departments would look to their university as the major (but not only) market for their research, courses and consultation activities. This could be an area in which a degree of marketization, whose problems would need careful consideration, would be preferable to the direct command chain that presently exists. It could provide a degree of critical distance and therefore independence from the institutions they are concerned to develop. It could also provide the research capacity building that is much needed if the development of universities is to be grounded in serious enquiry rather than merely responsive to immediate external pressures.

Such an approach would present universities with many challenges, requiring a degree of trust and confidence at a time when both are under threat. It would also require, and could create, a sense of shared purpose concerning the role of the university in society. Universities would have to consider very carefully the question: can they afford to subject their own practices to serious critique?

Conclusion

Academic development is a contested field of work. There are different ways of conceiving its theoretical and disciplinary base. Much thought, over the last ten years, has gone into attempting to clarify the identity of academic developers. If their work is to be seen in terms of critical engagement, rather than practical training, it offers exciting possibilities as different disciplines confront, collaborate and critique each other in an emerging conversation.

Problems of the identity of academic developers and the disciplinarity of their work, however, need to be understood in terms of institutionalized power. If academic development is to have a relationship with the university characterized by service that is critical rather than compliant, then it needs a degree of independence. In the short term, narrow and immediate interests may be met by compliant development. But in the longer term, universities need academic development that is prepared to confront difficult questions and entertain unpopular conclusions. This demands an approach to enquiry that embodies academic freedom.

Such an approach to academic development would challenge the university's capacity to manage its work. Can it afford to cast a critical perspective on its own practices?

The approach I have adopted in this chapter puts a high degree of emphasis on the interdisciplinary nature of critical engagement. This can also be a means by which the academic community gains integrity in the face of fragmentation. But how does interdisciplinarity work? What actually happens when different disciplines relate to each other? Is it even possible for those from one disciplinary way of thinking even to understand those of another? It is to such questions that I turn in the next chapter, with a focus more especially on the research aspects of enquiry.

7

Interdisciplinarity

The true voyage of discovery consists not in seeking new lands, but in
seeing with new eyes.

(Proust 1934)

The bones of the problem

I have made some rather large claims for interdisciplinarity. I suggested in
Chapter 2 that interdisciplinary research can involve the kind of contestation that opens up new and critical understandings, as accepted ideas and
identities are challenged. In the last chapter I argued that interdisciplinary
conversation can provide an opportunity for academics from different disciplinary backgrounds to learn from each other about their academic
practice. Moreover, if the university is to relate to the wider society it serves,
then it must engage across the boundaries between disciplines as well as the
boundaries between higher education and that wider society. In these ways,
at least, the enquiring university needs and welcomes interdisciplinarity.
Crossing boundaries is an important feature of engagement in the
enquiring university.

Such claims need careful consideration. What exactly is meant by interdisciplinarity in this context? How, if at all, is it possible and under what
circumstances does it lead to critical questioning? While interdisciplinary
enquiry sounds very well in theory, can it work in practice? How can
interdisciplinary work be enriched by the variety of its disciplinary languages rather than degenerate into a Tower of Babel as competing disciplinary perspectives fail to understand, or even listen to, each other?
These are the kinds of questions I shall now explore.

Davidson (2004) draws our attention to a legal wrangle that is 'an
enlightening example of interdisciplinary debate' involving conflicting
values in interdisciplinary engagement (p. 299). This wrangle is worth
exploring in some detail as it highlights, in a somewhat dramatic form,

some of the difficulties to be encountered when different disciplinary positions clash.

In July 1996 a skeleton, estimated to be 9200 years old, was discovered near Kennewick in the state of Washington. Reported in the *New York Times*, it was claimed that the Caucasoid nature of these remains added credence to theories that some early inhabitants of North America came from European stock. Further investigation of the remains was needed to confirm this idea.

Native American Indians saw it differently. If this individual is truly over 9000 years old, they argued, it only substantiates the theory that the skeleton is American Indian rather than European. From their oral histories they know that their people have been part of the land since the beginning of time. They reject the claim of some scientists who say the bones need to be studied further to provide evidence of American Indian history. As American Indians, they already know their history. It is passed on to them through their elders and through their religious practices (Egan 1999). They don't need scientists to tell them.

Rebecca Tsosie, a professor of law who serves on the Supreme Court of Justice for Fort McDowell Yavapai Nation Supreme Court, rejected the scientists' hypothesis, saying: 'It would be only too convenient to find that Native Americans are merely another "immigrant" group with no special claim to lands within the United States' (Lee 1999). Native American Indian understanding of the past has been disadvantaged in other ways, Tsosie said. She calls scientists 'secular priests' in a culture driven by values of knowledge and progress, and argues that American Indian oral traditions and beliefs don't have to bow to science. If the controversy boils down to a disagreement over who settled America – and that shows no hope of ever being resolved, even by scientists who disagree on what 'evidence' counts – then presumably American Indian theories on this should be entitled to as much weight as scientific theories, Tsosie said. For 'western science', according to Tsosie, 'gives us a way of knowing the world, a noble goal, but it's not the only way to establish something as the truth' (Wilford 1999).

American courts debated the question of whether or not the bones should be excavated by archaeologists against the wishes of the Indian groups who claim the right to protect the final resting places of their ancestors.

After nine years and several court rulings, the bones are in a Seattle museum at the time of writing. Scientists have been permitted to study them since a court ruling of 2004. But at a Senate Indian Affairs Committee hearing in July 2005, it was still not finally decided whether a genetic link would have to be established between Kennewick Man and present-day Native American Indians in order for them to be turned over to the Indians for burial (Blumenthal 2005).

As in many interdisciplinary disagreements, the difficulty of resolving the competing claims of the scientists and the American Indians is reflected in the different meanings given to the terms of the debate. The perception of the indigenous peoples that they had always been there is not necessarily inconsistent with the claim of the DNA specialists that a migration had occurred. The 'populations' and 'races' of the scientific account is not the same as a 'people' of oral history. Indeed, the very statement that 'our people have always been part of this land' is a complex assertion of identity that actually has little to do with DNA and matters of migration. Nor is the relationship between DNA and race agreed. From the Native American Indian point of view, even if archaeologists were to establish that the bones were of Caucasian origin (as determined by DNA), this would not be inconsistent with their being Indian. Scientific knowledge would therefore have nothing new to offer them and thus could not justify disrespecting their ancestors.

Now what we have here might be seen as a contest between two cultures, or between two epistemologies. Drawing on Foucault's idea of a 'regime of truth', disciplines may be seen as 'essential structures for systematising, organising and embodying the social and institutional practices upon which both coherent discourse and the legitimate exercise of power depend' (Lenoir 1993: 73). According to a definition such as this, the oral historians of Indian America and the scientists might be seen as representing different disciplines. The problem is, how are we to adjudicate between their different accounts and claims?

Interdisciplinary dispute

The idea of interdisciplinary collaboration, or interdisciplinarity, in this case, seems to be somewhat problematic. It is difficult to see how the court could have reached a decision without giving preference to either the American Indian or the archaeological set of structures. What seemed to be at stake here was not just a decision about a collection of bones, but a worldview.

Richard Dawkins, Professor of the Public Understanding of Science at Oxford University (UK), was critical of the sympathy in the USA for the American Indian claims regarding their ancestry and the sacredness of the bones. He views this as a consequence of a 'voguish fad' which holds science to be 'only one of many cultural myths' (Dawkins 1998: 18–19) which had no special claim over American Indian oral history. It is worth bearing in mind, however, that the 'voguish fad' that science provides only one way of understanding, or 'storying', the world (and thus of deciding upon the significance of the bones) resonates well with the writings of many scholars including some, such as Rorty (1982) and Feyerabend (1975), who have had a particular interest in the philosophy of science.

My purpose here is not to argue for one side or the other in the dispute over the bones, or over the wider question of whether scientific method is universal or culturally specific. Rather I want to acknowledge that discussions of interdisciplinarity raise questions not only about difference in areas of expertise and knowledge, but about the difference in the very nature of what counts as a claim to knowledge or expertise. Dawkins's 'voguish fads' and 'cultural myths' are typical of the terms of abuse that signify the culture wars and a breakdown in understanding across disciplinary boundaries, rather than a struggle for critical interdisciplinarity.

One does not need to look at such a dramatic case as the bones of Kennewick Man in order to see such interdisciplinary strife. Drawing upon his book *The Two Cultures* (Snow 1959), C. P. Snow argued in his 1959 Rede Lecture that there was a gulf of mutual incomprehension between literary intellectuals and scientists. Things have changed since 1959. With university research funding now increasingly directed towards science and technology, power within university culture is more strongly concentrated in the sciences than in the humanities. Thus, in his 2005 Reith Lectures, Sir Alec Broers, a prominent engineer and past Vice Chancellor of Cambridge University, was able to claim 'the triumph of technology' (Broers 2005). However, any claim that the gulf of incomprehension has been bridged by this Reith Lecture has been rejected by some (Raffle 2005).

Where interdisciplinary dispute is as extreme as in the story of Kennewick Man, and the regimes of truth are so far apart, how can some accommodation be made? If, as Lenoir suggests, we understand disciplines to have their own legitimating structures, then the only approach to resolving the issue is with reference to some further, superordinate set of legitimating structures to which both parties would consent. But this would amount to an appeal to, or the creation of, a new discipline rather than a case of interdisciplinarity.

The story of Kennewick Man certainly presents a somewhat extreme case. Even where there is no disagreement about the fundamental status of scientific reasoning, however, reaching consent across disciplinary boundaries can be difficult. In a study of the emergence of the interdisciplinary field of chemical engineering in French higher education, for example, the coming together of the two constituent disciplines, chemistry and engineering, involved a passionate 'war of words' (Detrez and Grossetti 1998). Significantly, in a later reflection upon this development and that of other cross-disciplinary engineering fields, Grossetti showed how interdisciplinary struggle was part of the process by which computer science and speech sciences also emerged to become autonomous disciplines (Grossetti 2005). Indeed, he suggests that the process of interdisciplinary engagement in science is a natural part of the development of disciplines. It expresses the critical and dynamic nature of disciplinary life. Disciplines, from this perspective, are not so much fixed regimes of truth but dynamic systems whose boundaries shift as research and teaching from different fields is drawn into new relationships in order to respond to new social needs.

This coming together of different disciplines to produce new disciplines is not only possible in the sciences. In the case of feminist scholarship and women's studies, Pryse (1998) argues that when interdisciplinarity combines the insights of two or more fields of study it can produce new fields.

She goes on to argue that such new fields bring to visibility previously suppressed knowledge. While her concept of 'suppressed knowledge' is perhaps particular to a feminist (rather than, say, Freudian) theory, the idea that interdisciplinarity can lead to new forms of knowledge is not uncommon in the humanities as well as the sciences.

This view seems to support that of the philosopher Heidegger (1977) who, in a short essay arguing the need for reflection on the inner dynamics of contemporary science, points out the mysterious way in which science depends on both disciplinarity and interdisciplinarity.

It appears, then, that when disciplinary cultures intersect, their differences may be irresoluble and collaboration impossible; or difficulties may be surmountable and lead to new fields of enquiry or disciplines. As with many intellectual endeavours, the difficulty involved in bringing together different disciplines, either to form a new field or simply to work on a specific project, can be a measure of the significance of the collaboration. The most valuable innovations in academic life are often the most hard won. Interdisciplinary work, as Martin Mueller put it from his perspective as a literary critic, is most difficult but also most productive when it involves the collision of strongly articulated disciplinary ethnicities (Mueller 1989).

Despite these difficulties in bringing together different disciplines, the term 'interdisciplinary' has become a buzzword in universities over the last fifteen years or so.

This enthusiasm for interdisciplinarity often emphasizes the value of bringing together different kinds of knowledge and skill, usually in order to solve a problem. The Genome Project is often seen in this light. The accounts of institutions keen to be perceived at the leading edge of problem-solving research also display a commitment to interdisciplinarity. The problems, however, are often viewed primarily in terms of the management of intellectual resources. Interdisciplinarity is seen as contributing to the expansion of knowledge and the need for universities to provide for the economy by directing its research towards practical problems. Thus, for example, a programme of an international conference held by the Canadian Association of Graduate Studies (CAGS 2005) emphasized that training in transdisciplinary research is vital to the promotion of innovation for social and economic advancement. This is part of a wider concern for collaboration, particularly in the sciences, which has developed since at least 1993 (Smith 2001: 137).

Multi-, inter- and transdisciplinarity

A further reason to view the current enthusiasm for interdisciplinarity with some caution arises from the multitude of different terms that are used to describe work across disciplinary boundaries. There is little articulation of what the different terms mean and how they differ. While 'interdisciplinary', 'multidisciplinary' and 'transdisciplinary' are common enough, 'pluridisciplinary', 'cross-disciplinary', 'hyperdisciplinary', 'intra-disciplinary' and 'meta-disciplinary' are all used in descriptions of post-graduate programmes and research.

In the light of the intense debate about the significance of the term 'discipline', this multiplicity of ill-defined prefixes is indicative of the confusion with which these matters are addressed. An attempt to distinguish between the uses of some of the various terms might help to clarify the situation and be more realistic about the potential of such innovation.

There appears to be no generally agreed definition of how the prefixes 'inter', 'multi' and 'trans' are used in this context. In the following summary I shall try to make some helpful distinctions, bearing in mind that any actual project or development is likely to have elements of each.

Multidisciplinarity and interdisciplinarity can be viewed as two ends of a continuum. At one extreme, multidisciplinary work is perhaps the simplest in its realization and conceptualization. It involves different disciplines working side by side in relation to a shared problem. The tasks involved in addressing the problem can, in principle at least, be divided up between the disciplines involved. While there will be some need to coordinate the separate activities, the assumption is that each discipline contributes from its own expertise on its own aspect of the problem. Those working in a multidisciplinary team may learn something of the work of other disciplines involved, but their own expertise is not challenged, nor would they challenge that of other participating disciplines. Thus the fundamental concepts of each discipline, its normal practices and methods are largely unquestioned by those in the collaborating disciplines. Respect for disciplinary expertise is a fundamental prerequisite of multidisciplinary teams.

The difficulties involved in such collaboration are primarily ones of managing the coordination of tasks and boundaries between them, rather than disputing disciplinary assumptions. While different disciplinary cultures are involved, the assumption is that these differences can be managed through the separation of responsibilities in which professional boundaries remain, as far as possible, uncontested. Such multidisciplinary collaboration is common in professional groups involving health and social work. For example, nurses, social workers, general practitioners and psychotherapists address such problems as the rehabilitation of stroke patients in multi-disciplinary teams (SIGN 2002).

At the other end of the continuum, interdisciplinary collaboration takes place where the problem is not divisible. It is investigated, as a whole, from the standpoints of the different disciplinary perspectives. This naturally leads to a range of different theoretical positions and underlying assumptions which need to be challenged and negotiated between the different disciplinary perspectives. Elsewhere in this book I have used the term 'critical interdisciplinarity' to draw attention to this feature of challenge and negotiation that is distinctive here, rather than in multidisciplinary work.

The term 'critical interdisciplinarity' appears to have been pioneered by Kroker (1980), a scholar of Canadian studies and later related to the critical theory of Horkheimer (1972). It has been adopted by some American feminist writers (such as Pryse 1998), particularly in addressing cultural boundaries. In relation to the study of higher education specifically, it was developed by Barnett (1997). Their rather different accounts all emphasize the dialectical and reflexive nature of critical interdisciplinarity that takes place when different disciplinary approaches contest each other's assumptions and ideological underpinnings. In the context of the theme of this book, critical interdisciplinarity is thus seen as a site of contestation between different perspectives in the attempt to come to new understandings.

Interdisciplinary work therefore often raises difficulties at the level of language and concepts. The idea of 'a people' in the Kennewick Man case meant one thing to archaeologists and another to Native American Indians. In interdisciplinary research and teaching even more fundamental terms become contested.

One such term is 'evidence'. The concept of evidence is arguably the most fundamental concept in all disciplinary enquiry. As the philosopher Jeremy Bentham pointed out, 'the field of evidence is no other than the field of knowledge itself' (Bentham 1810: 2). What counts as evidence, and how it is valued, varies across disciplines. Thus, for example, in health policy the randomized control trial (RCT) provides the 'gold standard' of evidence, while particular cases are viewed as merely anecdotal and of little evidential value. For a historian, on the other hand, no such trials are possible, evidence is invariably a particular event, document or artefact. The different ways in which the concept of evidence is approached is often therefore at issue in interdisciplinary work.

Problems concerning the different meanings and uses of 'evidence' and 'facts' in different fields of enquiry are the subject of considerable research. A research project at the London School of Economics (LSE 2003) focuses on how well evidence travels between and within disciplines and examines why evidence considered acceptable in one context retains or loses its status as evidence in another. Another, at University College London (UCL 2003), addresses the issue by attempting to advance a conceptual and methodological framework for a science of evidence, or evidence science. According to Schum (2001), evidence, and the ways it is handled, shares certain common features regardless of the phenomena to which it relates. Where this is so, it would certainly facilitate interdisciplinary enquiry.

Advancing this idea further, Twining proposes a 'field' of evidence as a multidisciplinary field in its own right, although it might be closer to the term 'interdisciplinary' as I am using it. Significantly, he finds the term 'evidence' preferable to 'evidence science', 'for the latter might carry some association with the dubious idea of disciplinary "autonomy"; it may also suggest that the subject belongs to the "hard" more than the "soft" disciplines, rather than at their interface' (Twining 2003: 91). Moreover, if the term 'science' is appropriate in this context, it presumably means science in the widest sense of sustained intellectual enquiry, rather than in the narrower sense that is applied to the natural sciences. A possible confusion here arises because the term 'science' in the English language is often distinguished from arts and humanities. In most continental European languages, however, 'science' has the wider meaning of disciplined enquiry.

The interest and funding that has been directed towards the interdisciplinary possibilities of evidence arises from a perceived social need. Terrorist outbreaks in a number of countries gave prominence to the importance of evaluating intelligence (as a form of evidence) from different sources and different disciplines; policy makers in a range of professional fields are increasingly advocating evidence-based policy; new technologies such as DNA identification give rise to evidential questions. Such developments all point to the need for ways of assessing evidence which draw upon different disciplinary perspectives.

Grossetti (2005) claims that new disciplines often emerge as a consequence of interdisciplinary activity in response to a social need. If he is right, and if the current interest in evidence develops, it is possible that evidence science does indeed become a new discipline with its own disciplinary autonomy. But whether such autonomy would be 'dubious', as Twining suggests, might depend upon whether it maintains its dynamic as a consequence of continued engagement with its bordering disciplines, or becomes static and protects its new-found status behind disciplinary walls.

A difficulty which arises in any discussion of disciplines and interdisciplinary research concerns the disciplinary status of the discussion itself. How is one to make a judgement about any single discipline except from a disciplinary standpoint? This problem is acknowledged by Messer-Davidow (1993) in the introduction to her edited collection on the history and critical study of disciplines. She acknowledges that the studies in the volume are from the perspective of historical and critical studies. It is therefore not surprising to find they all take the broad view that disciplines emerge as social or cultural phenomena and that epistemological differences are consequent upon social formations. A philosophy of the disciplines, on the other hand, is likely to foreground the epistemology as the defining feature of a discipline.

This theoretical difficulty has very practical consequences in interdisciplinary collaboration. Difficulties in reaching agreement about, say, how evidence should be treated or what should count as significant evidence, arise because one has to adopt *some* standpoint, even where participants are prepared to adjust their own perspective. It might be thought that the standpoint should be determined by the nature of the problem to be addressed. However, different disciplines reflect different interests and therefore different formulations of the problem. This is why interdisciplinary projects typically involve an extensive negotiation, and sometimes break down, over different understandings of the nature of the problem.

Difficulties of this sort can lead to a third version of work across disciplinary boundaries: transdisciplinarity. Transdisciplinary approaches are based upon the idea that the very concept of the discipline is itself inappropriate, is outdated, or is a device to preserve special interests. Some feminist writers (such as Salvaggio 1992) view disciplinarity as a gendered and oppressive construction to be 'transgressed'. Others have argued that disciplines are an academic form of knowledge inappropriate for collaboration on real problems. Gibbons *et al.* (1994), for example, recommend new forms of knowledge which emerge in a context where collaborative university research engages with problems that are situated in the world outside academe. They call the 'transdisciplinary' knowledge that arises from this context Mode 2, distinguishing it from Mode 1 'disciplinary' knowledge associated with university work on academic problems.

The value of the transdisciplinary approach is that it emphasizes crossing boundaries and leaving behind familiar disciplinary structures and conventions. It also emphasizes the importance of open-mindedness in research that is innovatory and involves working with new people in new ways and on new problems. Conciliation rather than contestation becomes important as attempts are made to reach out across disciplinary boundaries.

The danger, however, is that in seeking to avoid interdisciplinary contestation transdisciplinarity can lead to the collapse or denial of the forms of critique that characterize the disciplines. It is as if the lowest common denominator is sought in order to reach consensus, rather than facing the challenges of disciplinary difference. For this reason such an approach may lack the depth of interdisciplinary work.

A transdisciplinary approach is inclined to view the disciplines as static structures whose boundaries need to be overcome, rather than dynamic structures that grow and change through engagement across disciplinary boundaries. From a transdisciplinary (Mode 2) perspective, the disciplines represent disciplinary rigidity. From the perspective of critical interdisciplinarity, however, transdisciplinarity lacks disciplinary rigour.

C. P. Snow (1959) uses the metaphor of Hadrian's Wall to indicate the division between artistic and scientific cultures. This metaphor can be extended to apply to the multi-, inter- and transdisciplinary approaches as I have described them. In multidisciplinary collaboration participants coordinate their activities and speak to each other across the walls that divide them. Interdisciplinary work involves the renegotiation and repositioning of the walls, with all the struggle that this inevitably involves. Transdisciplinary approaches envisage rising above the walls or perhaps knocking them down.

In practice, projects involving different disciplines are likely to use a combination of multi-, inter- and transdisciplinary approaches. While the interdisciplinary approach, as I have described it, involves the highest degree of critique and contestation, there is little value in a project in which critique and contestation between participants means that nothing is ever agreed. The story of Kennewick Man may appear (so far) to have contributed little to raising awareness of aboriginal rights or of the relationships between science and culture.

The discipline as a site of contestation

The situation is more complicated than this. The 'regimes of truth' or 'essential structures' of many disciplines are often hotly contested *within* disciplines. This is probably more especially so within the humanities and social sciences. There may even be more agreement between academics working in *different* disciplines than there is between members of the same discipline. As Amarglio *et al.* (1993) argue, for example, 'Marxian economic thought shares more concepts, approaches and methods – may have more discursive regularity – with Marxian literary theory than do Marxian economic thought and neo-classical economic theory' (p. 151). Thus if it is 'a regime of truth' or 'essential structures' that distinguish disciplines, then Marxist economists and Marxist literary theorists might be said to belong to the same discipline more than do Marxist economists and neo-classical economists.

Taking this one stage further, contestation between members of the same discipline about its essential structures can be seen as an important feature of a dynamic discipline. This was the view of the architect who said: 'Architecture is a discipline in which the question "What is architecture?" must always be a valid and live question. Once we stop asking that question the discipline is dead' (see p. 71). From this perspective it is not simply *inter*disciplinarity that represents a site of contestation, but that the discipline itself is, or should be, such a site. Contestation about the 'regimes of truth' and 'systematizing of structures' embodied in knowledge is then viewed as fundamental in *all* university intellectual work, not only for those working across the largely institutional boundaries represented by the disciplines. Thus interdisciplinarity is nothing particularly new. It reminds us of the contested nature of knowledge and the continual need to challenge one's own assumptions and be aware of how one's standpoint might be viewed by those who do not share it. Perhaps such a reminder is particularly important in a context where knowledge has come to be viewed as a commodity to be delivered rather than the dynamic subject of scholarship.

At a Canadian university seminar, the development of interdisciplinary study in higher education was likened to curriculum integration in schools, which has intensified in Canada since 1985 (Panayotidis 2001: 7). It is not currently fashionable in the UK, however, where the National Curriculum and over-emphasis upon testing and target setting has succeeded in fragmenting the curriculum within disciplinary confines. Things were different a generation ago. In the period 1965–75, books such as *The Integrated Day in the Primary Classroom* (Brown and Precious 1968) recommended an approach in which children explore across disciplinary boundaries. Such open forms of learning were supported by the influential government-sponsored Plowden Report (CACE 1967), which encouraged project work drawing together different disciplinary or curriculum areas. This was also underpinned by prominent educational philosophers at the time such as Dearden (1968). This so-called 'progressive' approach to primary education was, however, rejected by policy makers who followed the UK Prime Minister Callaghan's famous speech at Ruskin College in October 1976. This argued that such progressive approaches undermined disciplinary rigour, the basics or the three Rs.

Thus moves towards integrated forms of study at primary school level are at best recommended for their emphasis upon critical, questioning or dialogical approaches, and at worst accused of lacking disciplinary rigour and being academically lightweight. We find an awareness of exactly the same problem in interdisciplinary work in higher education. Thus, the President of Stanford University (USA), in his address on 'The Vital Role of Multidisciplinary Scholarship' (Hennessy 2002), felt the need to reject the claim that interdisciplinary scholarship was academically lightweight. His rejection, however, was supported by little argument.

Further parallels might be drawn between the enthusiasm for the 'integrated day' during the 1970s in UK primary education (and its subsequent demise through the 1980s and 1990s) and the current enthusiasm for interdisciplinary research and teaching in higher education. These are similar to those explored in relation to skills (see Chapter 4). Both emphasize generic skills and more integrated forms of enquiry. These can be seen as responses of the educational system to demands that education and knowledge construction should be more closely aligned with social and economic needs. They are both critical of a rigidity and narrowness that have tended to characterize academic education and disciplinary research. In reacting to this criticism, however, they risk undermining the disciplinary knowledge that forms the basis of criticism. Both have been initiated by enlightened progressivism, yet risk being undermined by narrow pragmatism.

My interest, then, in exploring the possibilities of interdisciplinary research (and teaching) is not so much to advocate interdisciplinary work indiscriminately, with its various interpretations and contradictions, but rather to examine the potential of interdisciplinary study for critical dialogue.

This potential, however, is limited by a number of constraints that hold up interdisciplinary work. I shall now consider these constraints and opportunities for overcoming them, drawing upon a range of experiences and studies. These include the UK-based *Evidence, Inference and Enquiry* research programme (UCL 2003), which is in its early stages, and the USA-based National Research Council 2005 survey, *Facilitating Interdisciplinary Research* (National Academies 2005), which is probably the most wide-scale survey of views about interdisciplinary research.

Constraints and opportunities

Valuing interdisciplinary research

There is a general impression that funders have little regard for inter-disciplinary research proposals. Yet most research funding councils have explicitly sought submissions for such research. This is likely to be because individuals who have experience of interdisciplinary work are rarely to be found on panels judging proposals. There is an inbuilt conservatism. Academic work has traditionally been defined in narrowly disciplinary terms: the referees of research proposals have little interdisciplinary experience to draw upon. There is thus a danger that critical judgements that proposals lack disciplinary rigour may, at times, mask an underlying conservatism and inexperience. Lack of interdisciplinary research experience amongst referees means that there is little ability to judge what kind of inter-disciplinary research is likely to lead to opening up new and challenging opportunities rather than merely dilute disciplinary rigour. Funders should actively seek referees with an interdisciplinary background.

Journal publication

The problem manifests itself in a somewhat different way in relation to publication. The number of interdisciplinary journals has risen rapidly in order to meet the increased interest in interdisciplinary research. However, with a few exceptions (such as *Science* and *Nature*), interdisciplinary journals lack the prestige and impact of single-discipline journals (National Academies 2005: 139). As a consequence, academics and research students are less likely to receive professional advancement by publishing in inter-disciplinary journals. At the same time, submissions to disciplinary journals from the boundaries of interdisciplinary research are readily rejected by those committed to what Becher (1989) calls the 'disciplinary ideology', which is ever concerned to defend its boundaries. It seems again that despite the current rhetoric of university managers and external funders to promote interdisciplinarity, the established university culture of academic journals may well inhibit it. This could be viewed as a proper concern to defend disciplinary knowledge from increasing commodification and the associated undermining of disciplinary integrity. But more often it is likely to be the consequence of inbuilt conservatism. Journal editors might give more attention to identifying possible members of editorial boards who have experience working at and across the boundaries of their subject area.

Research assessment

In the UK, the Research Assessment Exercise (RAE) has compounded this effect. The National Academies Policy Advisory Group reported in 1996 on the research capability of the university system (the Harrison Report) that 'the RAEs tend to disadvantage interdisciplinary research' (NAPAG 1996: 18). There is little evidence that this problem was addressed in either the subsequent 2000 RAE or the plans for the 2008 RAE. Given the discussion above, however, of the varied and often inarticulate notions of what is meant by 'interdisciplinary research', it may well be that such work is supported, or not, depending upon the definition employed. In this rather confusing situation, academics were advised to submit interdisciplinary work to the single discipline to which it was most closely related and also to suggest a second, related, panel for consideration (Geuna and Martin 2001: 7). Such a procedure is unlikely to advance the prestige of interdisciplinary research and is likely to confirm the suspicion that it lacks disciplinary rigour.

One possible solution is to view interdisciplinary activity as a specialism in its own right. The difficulty then, however, would be that new specialisms would emerge and fade with such rapidity that it would be difficult to capture and measure their achievements within such an inherently conservative structure as the RAE. It is of the nature of innovation that it is difficult to evaluate until it is no longer innovative.

Recruitment and promotion

The problems encountered in attracting funds for interdisciplinary research, publishing research findings and research assessment obviously impact negatively upon recruitment and promotion. Nevertheless, while a concern for career advancement may incline academics towards keeping within the safe confines of their discipline, many of the most exciting and influential intellectuals have been those who have made new connections between fields of enquiry. Interdisciplinary research may be difficult, but the rewards of conducting exciting work across boundaries can, in the longer term, lead to considerable advancement. As the Chief Executive of the Arts and Humanities Research Board noted: 'Many of the most exciting areas of research lie between and across the boundaries of traditional disciplines or subjects' (AHRC 2004).

Departmental boundaries

Whatever sense we are to make of the concept of a discipline, in the light of the preceding discussion, it appears that disciplinary boundaries and

departmental boundaries are not the same thing. Interdisciplinary collaboration within departments can be as difficult as working across departmental boundaries. While the fragmentation described in Chapter 5
disables communication between colleagues, organizational structures
exacerbate this effect. One consequence is a lack of reflective space in
which the kind of conversations can take place that stimulate critical forms
of interdisciplinarity. As a consequence, interdisciplinarity is often seen as
presenting a management problem which is open to managerial solutions,
rather than an intellectual one. This tends to promote instrumental rather
than critical forms of interdisciplinary collaboration. Given the difficulty
that university managers have of setting up interdisciplinary institutional
structures, interdisciplinarity is often best developed from the bottom up.

Risk aversion

Stimulating interdisciplinary work from the bottom up is risky, however.
One often needs to keep trying in the face of conflicting possibilities.
Interdisciplinary collaboration inevitably faces the possibility of redundancy
and the risk of failure. The dominant regime of accountability discourages
risk taking, particularly when its methods of measurement are disciplinarily
based. These risks are perhaps most sharply felt by research students. Feller
(2005) gives an illuminating account of how even in a department known
for its interdisciplinary work, research students were encouraged not to
pursue research that was too interdisciplinary, because of the risks involved.
While senior academics may be able to afford to risk the difficulties of
interdisciplinary research, less secure junior academics and students should
play it safe. Such an approach perpetuates the lack of interdisciplinary
PhDs. Indeed, where students do follow an interdisciplinary route to a PhD,
there is some evidence that this is not a satisfactory route to gaining an
academic appointment (Feller 2005: 6).

Disciplinary insecurity

Some disciplines are more clearly defined than others. It is commonly held,
for example, that the natural sciences tend to be more confident in their
disciplinary status than disciplines in the arts, humanities and professionally
related areas. It is important to remember, however, that even physics only
became an established discipline in the mid-nineteenth century and some
of the boundaries between the natural sciences seem much less secure now
than they did a generation ago. It was claimed by people who identified
their discipline as being less secure (English literature, education) that this
quality actually encouraged attempts to seek collaborative relationships with
others from different disciplines (Rowland 2002b).

One might expect, however, quite the opposite tendency: that insecure disciplines are, for that very reason, concerned to protect and defend their boundaries against incursion. The development of psychology as a discipline during the early nineteenth century might be seen as an instance of a new discipline which was concerned to establish itself as a natural science and thus defended itself from more humanistic forms of enquiry.

Perhaps a distinction here needs to be made between insecurity that arises from a concern to keep 'regimes of truth' open to reinterpretation, and insecurity that arises from a concern to establish an emergent discipline within a wider field of disciplines competing for resources and status. The former sort of insecurity is characteristic of the established arts and humanities. At its best it represents a preparedness to listen and keep open the possibilities of challenge; at its worst it leads to continuing internecine dispute between conflicting ideological positions. The latter form of insecurity is more commonly associated with emergent disciplines in the sciences. At best this is a proper concern to develop rigorous methods, at worst a narrow-minded defence of boundaries. It is sometimes difficult to have enough confidence in one's disciplinary perspective in order to set it aside and listen to the different stories of others.

Social need

Drawing upon the work of Grossetti (2005), effective interdisciplinarity often results from the identification of a social need which academics interpret and respond to. Social needs are, however, often open to different interpretations and in consequence different relationships between the constituent disciplines. An interesting example of this is in the field of medical humanities in the UK. In an announcement in the *British Medical Journal* of a new journal, *Medical Humanities*, Evans and Greaves (1999) articulated two very different conceptions of the new field.

> An 'additive' view, whereby an essentially unchanged biomedicine is softened in practice by the sensitised practitioner and an 'integrated' view, whereby the nature, goals, and knowledge base of clinical medicine itself are seen as shaped by the understanding and relief of human bodily suffering. This more ambitious view entails that the experiential nature of suffering be brought within the scope of medicine's explanatory models, if necessary by reappraising those models.
>
> (Evans and Greaves 1999: 1216)

Here the 'more ambitious' interpretation demanded a critical relationship between the disciplines involved as the humanities would be 'reappraising those models' of biomedicine. While the 'additive' view aims to improve the situation by 'softening' practice through the introduction of humanities, the 'integrated' one challenges the knowledge base of clinical medicine by introducing the insights from humanities into its field. It therefore questions the very basis upon which judgements about improvement are made.

The 'additive' view corresponds to what I have called multidisciplinarity, while the more ambitious 'integrated' view corresponds to inter-disciplinarity.

Bolton (2003) argued in the pages of *The Lancet* for this more 'integrated' or interdisciplinary view of medical humanities which would challenge medical judgement. But five years after the launch of *Medical Humanities*, leaders in the field were still asking whether the field was multidisciplinary or interdisciplinary (Evans and Macnaughton 2004). The unresolved question here was not simply a matter of research management or meth-odology, but concerned the purpose of medical humanities. Is the need to soften clinical practices or to question the basis of medical judgement? The former required a multidisciplinary or 'additive' approach; the latter an interdisciplinary or 'integrated' one.

Thus the potential for critical interdisciplinarity in work across dis-ciplinary boundaries depends to a large extent on how the social need is interpreted. Where this involves challenging existing assumptions and practices, then critical interdisciplinarity is likely to be appropriate. Critical needs demand critical methods.

Conclusion

A major theme of this book has been that the university exists within a tension or dialectic between compliance and contestation. This tension is reflected in the ways that university knowledge is constructed. The very term 'discipline' denotes compliance, in this context within a well-grounded framework of methods, purposes and practices. But progress involves reaching beyond, testing the boundaries and stepping into uncharted ter-ritory. Close interaction between disciplines raises one possibility for con-testing and stepping beyond disciplinary boundaries.

This chapter indicates that interdisciplinary research is complex. The same applies to teaching. At one extreme it can involve contestation between conflicting perspectives to such an extent that little is achieved and collaboration and learning becomes impossible. At the other extreme, multidisciplinarity can present no more than a management problem: participants work beside each other but within their safe disciplinary boundaries; the different ways of thinking do not impact upon each other. Between the two extremes there is a possibility for spaces in which really challenging and innovative work can take place.

Institutional constraints and conservative academic practices, however, have the effect of reinforcing compliance and encouraging work within safe disciplinary boundaries. These limitations need to be addressed if inter-disciplinary work is to overcome its inherent difficulties and flourish. It involves being prepared to listen to the unfamiliar and often conflicting ideas from different backgrounds. In the most general terms, it raises the question of how researchers, students and teachers learn from each other as they engage in a shared subject matter. Its success depends upon the ability to enquire and learn together. This is what I want to consider more closely in the next chapter.

8

Enquiry and the reintegration of teaching and research

Man conceives a human nature much stronger than his own, and sees
no reason why he cannot acquire such a nature. Thus he is urged to
seek the means that will bring him to such a perfection, and all that can
be the means that will bring him to such perfection is called a true
good, while the supreme good is to arrive at the enjoyment of such a
nature, together with other individuals, if possible.

(Spinoza 1992)

Introduction

Earlier chapters have argued the need for intellectual space in which
enquiry can ameliorate the effects of fragmentation, explore the creative
potential of disciplinary difference, and gain a clearer sense of the purposes
of higher education. Academic enquiry takes place in a tension between
compliance and contestation. In the present situation, where compliance is
the stronger force acting upon the higher education system, there is a
particular need to emphasize the critical purposes of higher education.
Without this critical function universities will fail to provide a service to
society that is educational.

So far I have used the term 'enquiry' in a somewhat all-embracing way, to
indicate teaching, learning, research and all forms of engagement directed
towards increasing understanding. In this chapter I want to elaborate this
concept. Universities are in the business of teaching and research and while
each may be seen as a form of enquiry, academics' experience of teaching is
normally somewhat different from their experience of research. Referring
to both teaching and research under the category of 'enquiry' can serve to
point out the similarities. But it fails to address the difference which is a very
prominent aspect of academic life. I thus want to consider the basis of
enquiry more closely, how this impacts upon the relationships between

teaching and research, and how it can serve to bring the two into more symbiotic relationships.

'When I recall the teachers that most influenced me, what I remember is their love of the subject, their desire to engage me in their enthusiasm and their sense of the excitement of discovery.' Something along these lines has been said to me many times. So the question 'is there a close relationship between teaching and research?' seems to be almost rhetorical when applied to the higher branches of learning. How could one enjoy teaching without being fascinated by the subject and wanting to find out more about it?

Yet when we consider the ways teaching and research are dominated by relationships of power, vested interests and purposes apart from the search for understanding, the question ceases to be rhetorical. It challenges institutions to create and protect genuinely open enquiry where research or teaching can be mutually enhancing.

That is the conclusion I would like to arrive at. But there is also an opposing perspective: that teaching and research are fundamentally different activities. Research consists in the discovery or creation of new knowledge whereas teaching is the passing on of established understanding. From this point of view teaching and research may require different kinds of spaces and they may not serve to enhance each other.

The difference between these two perspectives has much to do with how we understand the role of discovery in learning. If discovery is an important aspect of learning, as it is of research, then it could serve to link teaching and research: the space for discovery could be a requirement of each. This is a question of pedagogy. It concerns the relationship between knowledge, the knower and coming-to-know. It is also perhaps the most ancient of unresolved pedagogical problems: what is the relationship between discovery and instruction?

I therefore want to start this exploration by considering this pedagogical problem concerning the roles of discovery and instruction in learning. To do this, I shall give a historical sketch from a few of the many writers who have struggled with this problem since the times of Ancient Greece. My references will not be scholarly, or accompanied by critique, but will simply be to inform a conception of enquiry that might provide a link between instruction and discovery, and between teaching and research.

Reflections from the past

Plato is perhaps the most well-known and earliest exponent of what might be called discovery methods of teaching adults. Writing through the voice of his teacher, Socrates, Plato constructs a number of dialogues between Socrates and an interlocutor, often in the role of student. The Socratic Method, as it came to be known, was based upon the teacher posing only critical questions, rather than solutions, and in this fashion leading the student towards a better understanding of the subject in question. Of course, much of Socrates's questioning led his interlocutors to realize the falsity of their assumptions. But acknowledging one's ignorance is often a precondition for entertaining new ideas. It creates the space for new knowledge. Thus, for Plato, it was through Socratic questioning, rather than through instruction, that new understandings emerge in the adult learner.

This Socratic Method (see especially Plato's *Meno*) was based upon Plato's belief that life has a pre-bodily form in which the individual is fully acquainted with knowledge (or the Forms, as Plato would have said). It follows that learning is not so much a matter of teaching as of being reminded, or brought to an awareness, of this innate knowledge. Plato was particularly concerned here with mathematical and moral knowledge, which were the most important aspects of education in Athens. The teacher's task is then to prompt this reminiscence: the learner rediscovers the truth; the truth is, as it were, reborn. The term 'maieutic' (from the Greek maievtikos, meaning midwifery) is sometimes used to describe this Socratic Method, or dialectic, in which innate wisdom is elicited through critical questioning (Levin 1999).

While Plato's ideas about pre-bodily life and innate knowledge seem out of place today, even this brief account has some interesting parallels with modern thinking about learning. Chomsky's idea that the brain is genetically programmed with the ability to learn languages (Chomsky 1983) contains this Platonic idea of innateness which has implications for teaching. Carl Rogers's emphasis upon facilitation and student-centredness, as opposed to instruction (Rogers 1969), owes much to Socrates's maieutic method. And the importance that reflection is currently held to play in learning relates to the Platonic idea that knowledge and understanding is to be gained by questioning and thinking in depth about what we know, rather than by being presented with new facts.

We can thus see Plato's Socratic Method as being aimed at discovering, or perhaps more accurately uncovering, the truth, through critical dialogue. According to Plato this process was essential for learning, whether we conceive of this in terms of students learning from their Socratic teacher or in terms of the dialectical processes of researcher or thinker at the forefront of knowledge. What we might now think of as pedagogy (as applied to adults) and research methodology would not then have been distinct.

At the same time in Athens, however, there were others such as Isocrates, who was also a pupil of Socrates, who held a very different view about knowledge and learning. Isocrates was interested in persuasion or rhetoric rather than encouraging learners to discover the truth for themselves. 'Rhetoric', in its original meaning, is a persuasive argument designed to bring an audience over to the speaker's point of view.

The Ancient Greek rhetoricians were not so much scholars or academics as lawyers, diplomats and other powerful functionaries. Their 'learners', often those in positions of political power, they advised and persuaded through smooth talk. While their rhetoric might be dialogical (as in a court of law in which different viewpoints compete), its purpose was primarily practical rather than theoretical, and its form competitive rather than reflective or contemplative. The rhetorical approach thus indicates a pedagogy that is quite opposed to Plato's, closing down, rather than opening up, processes of discovery and theoretical understanding. Indeed, Plato's ideas are thought to have developed in reaction to the prominence of rhetoric at the time and in favour of a more dialectical approach.

While Plato's dialectic placed the emphasis upon the search for the truth, rhetoric was concerned with the correct ways of using words to formulate the truth. The Stoics, on the other hand, claimed that both were important 'sciences' (see, for example, Diogenes Laërtius 1895: XXXIV).

The present-day context is very different, but we can see how rhetoric also plays an important role in teaching today. Indeed, the university lecture might be seen primarily as a rhetorical device, or a form of instructional method, in which the lecturer persuades the students concerning the subject matter being presented. Taking this further, one might even see the idea of a discipline as being a structure of thinking formulated through rhetorical argument.

There was thus a conflict of views in ancient Greece between those who emphasized discovery through critical dialogue or dialectics, and those for whom practical needs were best served by instruction through rhetoric. This dispute has many parallels with contemporary debates about the value of involving students in discussion rather than lectures. The position of the Stoics, who saw that each had its place, is one to which most would consent today.

If we go forward nearly two thousand years to the sixteenth century, we can see a similar debate at the very beginnings of what has come to be termed the Enlightenment, following the break-up of Christian unity in Europe. The French writer Montaigne (1533–92) came from a wealthy family where he naturally took on such responsibilities as becoming the mayor of his town at a relatively early age. But in his mid-thirties, Montaigne decided to devote his life to independent study, scholarship and writing. At that time in Europe formal education was highly structured by scholastic and doctrinaire approaches. Students were expected to learn passages from Roman and Ancient Greek texts, translation from Latin and Greek was important in the curriculum, and subjects like grammar and logic were learnt formally through rules and procedures committed to memory. The Classics had become the subject of drill and conformity rather than enjoyment and enlightenment.

Montaigne reacted against this climate rather as Plato reacted against the sophists and rhetoricians. In his essay *Of the Education of Boys* (Montaigne 1935: 142–78), he puts forward a radically different view in which the curriculum is based upon activity arising from the learner's interests, rather like the 'active learning' and 'problem-based learning' of today. His view was that the scholastic forms of education prominent at the time produced students who knew a lot but did not know how to use their knowledge wisely. In sympathy, perhaps, with modern students who have suffered too many lectures, Montaigne says: 'I am not prepared to bash my brains for anything' (de Botton 2001: 157). Learning should be a pleasure for students, he argued. Students should not tolerate boredom and undue prominence should not be given to the difficult texts of dead authors. Montaigne himself quoted widely from classical texts, which he loved. He even adorned his library by carving 54 quotations from Ancient Roman and Greek writers into its wooden beams (Robertson 1935: xxviii). But he was appalled by the way teaching had become little more than drill and not a way to instil a love of Classics or any other subject.

The theme is taken up in the early eighteenth century, when Jean-Jacques Rousseau (1679–1778) argued that education should take place in an environment in which students learn to think for themselves rather than have their teachers do their thinking for them. Teachers should not just hand inherited orthodoxies down to their students. Again, this sounds very much like the kind of criticism that has been made of so-called 'traditional' methods of instruction.

At the turn of the twentieth century, John Dewey (1859–1952) developed the point further, arguing that education should not be the cramped study of other people's learning. He would have been familiar with the caricature of Mr Gradgrind from Charles Dickens' *Hard Times*, a satire of Victorian education a generation earlier in which the discipline of knowledge was intimately related to the brutal discipline of a rigidly hierarchical society. In contrast, he claimed that education had a democratic purpose.

In this sketch it is important to acknowledge the philosophical differences between these thinkers: the idealism of Plato, the romanticism of Rousseau, the pragmatism of Dewey. Such differences would be difficult to explain only in terms of the place and time of their writing. But underneath or alongside these differences is a shared concern to create an environment in which learners have the space to discover knowledge as a result of their own autonomous and critical participation, rather than cramped orthodoxy and didactic instruction. Of course, most would argue like the Stoics that instruction should play some part in learning. Even Plato believed that instruction played an important role in the education of young children. But each of these writers presents the view that the space for discovery needs to be emphasized in the face of a system or culture of education that collapses teaching into mere instruction and seems more concerned to discipline thought than to emancipate it.

Even if we can identify a proper balance between discovery and instruction, the relationship between the two presents problems. It needs to be understood if we are to create the kind of spaces in which teaching and research might productively relate to each other.

Intellectual love and the nature of enquiry

The concept of discovery is too narrow to encompass the richness of the kind of experiences, relationships, attitudes and values that underlie teaching and research in the university. For that, I want to develop a concept of enquiry that encompasses and extends beyond discovery. I shall suggest that intellectual love is its key component and that it forms a basis for both teaching and research.

Enquiry (quest for the truth from the Latin *quaere verum*) involves seeking. Pedagogically, perhaps the most important task of the teacher is to develop an atmosphere or an attitude in which students seek. Jerome Bruner (1966: 142) describes how the teacher attempts to 'become part of the student's internal dialogue' in order to develop such questioning. With adults specifically in mind, Radley (1980: 42) describes how this is a symmetrical process in which 'both student and tutor are engaged in a two way process of expressing what they are trying to formulate and grasping those things which the other person is indicating'. Like the Socratic dialogue referred to above, such a reflective dialogical stance leads learners to generate questions and become aware of what they don't know, but need to know. This might lead to an awareness of the need for instruction from a textbook, lecture, demonstration or whatever. Or it may lead to discovery from experimentation, data gathering and so on. Or it may simply lead to further open questioning and enquiry. The important issue here is not so much about whether instruction or discovery best promotes learning, but that either should emerge from genuine seeking on the part of the learner, that is, from enquiry.

The learner's enquiry thus provides the basis or ground for discovery and the motivation for learning from instruction. Without the questioning arising from the learner's enquiry, discovery is unlikely to emerge and instruction unlikely to be successful. I make fuller elaboration of this aspect of enquiry and relationship to professional development in *The Enquiring Tutor* (Rowland 1993).

Similarly, for the researcher, enquiry provides the ground for discovering new knowledge and the motivation for its scholarly dissemination. Such a description of research coincides with Stenhouse's definition: 'systematic enquiry made public' (Stenhouse 1980: 5).

Enquiry is thus a link between teaching and research. Teaching consists of instruction *in the context of enquiry*. Research publication (and other research outcomes) consists of scholarly dissemination *in the context of enquiry*. But what sustains enquiry? Why do researchers, teachers or learners enquire?

A colleague who taught dentistry explained to me how his teaching of dentistry was based upon one aim: to inspire in his students a love of dentistry (Carrotte 1994). As experience dentistry as little more than a necessary evil, his love of the subject was intriguing. But it soon became clear that this was similar to the love that historians, physicists and other academics have expressed and with which I find it easier to identify. This love of the subject characterizes their enquiry, whether that enquiry be directed at discovering new knowledge (research), or becoming more acquainted with what is already known (often referred to as scholarship), or imparting that knowledge to students (teaching).

It is difficult to speak of love. Definitions seem oddly out of place. Sometimes the word seems to mean nothing more than a positive feeling towards its object. At others its use appears to be merely an expression of sentiment. Yet it also represents the most significant form of human commitment possible. The significance of the term is highly context-dependent. The readiness and passion with which many academics claim that they love their subject, however, demands that we should at least be able to say something about the nature of this love which appears to be central to academic enquiry, rather than to dismiss it as mere sentiment or sloppy use of language. Such love may be an ideal which is often unrealized in practice. But it is helpful to consider the nature of this ideal before exploring its application in practice.

For the rationalist philosopher Spinoza (1632–77) the love of knowledge of God the Creator (*natura naturans*) and God as his creation, Nature (*natura naturata*), was the ultimate human characteristic. It is what brings man closer to God, in Spinoza's terms. This 'intellectual love' might therefore suggest an ideal basis for academic pursuit. As a pantheist, Spinoza believed that everything was an aspect of God: He, the Creator, cannot be separated from Nature that He created. Spinoza's intellectual love combines what modern-day psychologists would call the cognitive and the affective. It is for him the highest form of human happiness (Elwes 1955: xxviii–xxix). Unlike the Puritans at the time, who scorned the passions as being the source of human evil, Spinoza's intellectual love involved both intellectual thought and emotion, or self-motivated passion. Spinoza often distinguishes between the passions (such as lust) in relation to which we are passive, and the emotions (such as love) in relation to which we are active. In fact, the etymology of the terms 'passion' (suggesting passivity and suffering in the face of forces we are unable to control) and 'emotion' (suggesting a motivating force) indicates the distinction being made. For Spinoza it was important that individuals should become more aware of the feelings over which they have no control – the passions – and thereby gain a degree of control over them, transforming them into emotions. This insight foreshadows the psychoanalytic approach of Freud, some 250 years later.

My colleague's love of dentistry was, in Spinoza's terms, an emotion over which he exercised control rather than a passion that controlled him. Indeed, it would have seemed very peculiar if he had said 'I just can't help loving dentistry', as one might say 'I just can't help loving cream buns.' Academics may say they are 'passionate' about their subject, but in this context the word no longer carries its earlier association with passivity as implied by Spinoza's distinction. It is, indeed, an active love rather than a passive lust.

For Spinoza, intellectual love is the desire for knowledge of God, understood to be co-extensive with all existence. Thus, the desire to know more about dentistry or physics is, from Spinoza's point of view, a desire to know more about God. Since God is infinite, this search for knowledge is never complete. The more we know, however, the closer we come to Him. And the closer we come to God, the more we become identified with Him and take on His characteristics, in particular the characteristic of intellectual love. Intellectual love therefore gives rise, in principle, to a virtuous cycle of increasing knowledge of God leading to increasing intellectual love or desire to know more of God.

This ideal conception of intellectual love is useful in the more secular context of this discussion of enquiry and what it is to love one's subject. The object of intellectual love's desire, the subject matter, is never fully known. We may come to know better, but we can never come to know completely; we can find out what we wanted, but this leaves further questions for enquiry, further knowledge desired. Like the love of the lover who always desires greater intimacy with the loved one, so intellectual love always wants a more intimate acquaintance with the subject matter. Intellectual love, like personal love, is thus strengthened, rather than exhausted, by being expressed.

Intellectual love therefore provides an excellent basis for academic enquiry. Unlike other forms of enquiry (such as criminal investigation) it suggests a continuing and developing interest rather than one that becomes exhausted once the initial question has been answered. It might lead to an awareness of what is not known but needs to be known in order to answer one's question, or it may lead to changes of direction and focus of the enquiry as one becomes aware of new aspects of one's ignorance.

An awareness of one's own ignorance, like the realization of one's own error, is perhaps the most crucial moment of learning (as Plato had indicated through his Socratic dialogues). It creates the intellectual space for new knowledge. Whether this is provided by a teacher, a text, or by a colleague, such contributions to understanding are purposeful because they arise to meet the needs identified in the enquiry. Arising from a context of enquiry such contributions to knowledge serve the further development of enquiry.

Teachers with students or collaborating researchers involved in such enquiry acknowledge the subject matter's, or discipline's, existence beyond the sphere of their intimacy. The subject therefore always remains open to further interpretation, further questioning and new ways of knowing. Familiarity does not breed contempt but invites new avenues of exploration. Karl Popper's Searchlight Theory of Science adopts this view of the progress of science research as the asking of ever more significant questions. He contrasts this with his Bucket Theory of Science which views research as the cumulative addition of truths (Popper 1979). In relation to teaching, a parallel distinction is made by Paolo Freire (1972), who contrasts a critical or questioning approach to learning with the more traditional 'banking theory of learning'.

In the context of Spinoza's theology, intellectual love is an attribute of God. To the extent that it exists in humans, it is directed towards increasing knowledge of God. It is therefore an open rather than a secretive and jealous love.

Translating this into a secular context, intellectual love is inclusive rather than exclusive; it seeks to share rather than hoard. The idea of academics loving their subject but not wanting to share what they know with others would be incongruous. It would not be an instance of intellectual love. It may be an example of what Freud called 'epistemophilia' or Derrida has described as 'archive fever' (Derrida 1996): an obsessive–compulsive disorder more akin to lust than love.

Many well-known scientists have, of course, like Isaac Newton, been shy people (Gleick 2003) and many do not like talking about their work to large lecture halls of listeners. But it is inconceivable to imagine that, in circumstances and by means of their choosing, they would not want to share their knowledge with others.

I have begun to present a picture of enquiry motivated by a love of the subject matter as being at the centre of academic practice. In an academic environment, enquiry is a necessary condition for effective teaching and research. In that way, it suggests a link between them. The more intellectual love is expressed through research, the more it is strengthened. And the more it is strengthened, the greater can be its contribution to teaching. Thus, for our academic dentist, the more his love of dentistry is enhanced by his own enquiries into dentistry, the greater will be the intellectual love that inspires his teaching. This is not to suggest that teachers should teach students their particular specialism, but that their teaching is underpinned by the love that motivates their specialist research.

It does not follow from this that, even under ideal conditions, those who are best able to disseminate the products of their enquiry through publication would necessarily be best able to engage their students in enquiry. Other abilities are involved. Intellectual love is a necessary, but not sufficient, condition for effectiveness in research and teaching. The more it is enhanced, the greater will be the impact upon both.

Reformulating the link between teaching and research

The ideal I have so far presented does not necessarily portray what actually happens in practice. It does, however, provide a framework for interpreting observations and conclusions concerning research and policy into the matter of how teaching and research relate. A much-quoted (and often misquoted) conclusion of a meta-review of research into this relationship (Hattie and Marsh 1996) was that there was little correlation between those who are good teachers and those who are good researchers, and that this lack of relationship indicated a problem to be addressed. This research was quoted out of context in the UK government White Paper *The Future of Higher Education* (DfES 2003), which claimed that the lack of correlation justified a policy of further separating teaching and research. In fact the finding can equally be used to justify bringing them closer together, as the authors make clear. Our discussion suggests that research enhances intellectual love to the benefit of teaching, but it does not follow from this that there is a correlation between being a good teacher and a good researcher.

The lack of correlation between effective teaching and effective research is more likely to be the result of the weakness of a culture of enquiry in both teaching and research in higher education. The conclusion of many writers, such as Elton (2001), Brew (2001) and Boyer (1990), that teaching and research are more closely related when teaching follows an enquiry-based approach would be consistent with the framework offered here. So also would be the view that the common feature of both research and teaching is that they are both acts of learning (Brew and Boud 1995), inasmuch as learning can be a form of enquiry.

The strengthening of enquiry in higher education may do something to address the common complaints that many academic staff make that their students are no longer motivated by a love of their subject, and that research output is now driven by the demand to meet assessment. But this presents problems as long as discussions of higher education policy relating to both teaching and research are invariably predicated upon the assumption that the purpose of higher education is primarily to increase individual and social economic advantage. Under such extrinsic pressures, the intrinsic value of a love of knowledge, essential to enquiry, inevitably takes second place.

Were there to be greater public recognition that 'the primary purpose of education should not be the living that students will earn but the life they will lead' (Halsey *et al.* 1961), then enquiry based on intellectual love might be assured a prominent place.

Intellectual love requires the kind of space that does not readily submit to technical control and management. It cannot so easily give an account of itself in terms of the kinds of measures that readily translate into the league tables of a competitive market environment. Its value being intrinsic rather than instrumental, intellectual love is a way of being in the world rather than a means of producing outcomes. It is therefore vulnerable to an educational ethos that is increasingly driven by indicators of performance. For that is inclined to misconstrue a love of the subject matter as being inappropriate for a state-funded mass, rather than elite, system of higher education. The UK's Education Secretary in 2003 wrote that: 'the medieval concept of a community of scholars seeking truth' was not an appropriate basis for a modern university (see p. 2). The implication of such a statement is that the seeking of truth, and social value, are alternatives between which we have to choose rather than mutually enhancing values. Such a point of view is problematic, especially when the identification of what in fact *is* of social value is not at all clear and appears to be largely led by markets outside democratic control. To disparage truth seeking as a medieval monastic practice indicates an anti-intellectual value which has no space for enquiry founded upon intellectual love.

If, as I have argued, a culture of enquiry provides a link between teaching and research, then the weakening of enquiry would have a negative impact upon research as well as upon teaching. Has it?

A very strong argument concerning this question was presented to the Association of University Teachers in UK in 2002. Drawing upon observations of a range of prominent senior academics, this document identified ways in which the audit culture associated with research 'perverts research' and 'obstructs innovation' (Tagg 2002). A central part of their argument was based upon a sociological idea that parallels Heisenberg's uncertainty principle in physics, that is, that the attempt to measure something inevitably changes the value of that which is to be measured. Often referred to as 'Goodhart's Law' (Charles Goodhart was for several years Chief Adviser to the Bank of England), this states that in business organizations, as soon as government attempts to regulate any particular set of financial assets, these become unreliable as indicators of economic trends because financial institutions can easily identify new types of financial assets (Goodhart 1984).

According to McIntyre (2001), this same principle applies to the measurement of higher education's assets of teaching and research. In this case, the identification of certain indicators of research value (such as academic publications, research contract income) inevitably leads institutions and individuals to maximize their score on these items, regardless of the consequences elsewhere. Such an approach to audit is likely to show increased measures related to research or teaching merely because the actors have become adept at playing the game of maximizing their scores. The real purpose and value of new knowledge created by research is not always readily measurable and so an emphasis on maximizing scores takes attention away from the more important intellectual purposes of research. Thus, they argue, audit 'perverts' research and teaching.

Such forms of audit characteristically lead to unintended outcomes, as has often been observed. One of these is the elimination of risk that comes about as human action is transformed into technical production (Grundy 1992). As in the discussion of interdisciplinarity in the last chapter, the question of risk taking again becomes important. A preparedness to take risks is as fundamental a part of the dynamic of intellectual love as it is of personal love. It is through taking risks that greater intimacy can arise, new territories be encountered and trust built. In this way, accepted knowledge, understanding and methods can be challenged and disciplinary rigour enhanced. Furthermore, if higher education is to fulfil its economic and social purposes it must be prepared to take the kinds of risk that necessarily accompany innovation. The risk-averse culture associated with audit stifles innovation and undermines professional trust.

In the context of our discussion of intellectual love, Tagg's use of the term 'perversion' to describe the impact of the culture of audit upon research is apposite. For the perversion of intellectual love implies the prostitution of intellectual endeavour. The love of knowledge is then replaced by a lust in the competitive knowledge game. Enhancing the relationships between teaching and research may require us to resist the forms of perversion that infect both.

Conclusion

I have offered a conception of university enquiry that places the love of knowledge at its centre. Although I relate this idea back to Spinoza, it is also the inspiration of the eighteenth-century Enlightenment, which linked the search for knowledge with emancipation and democracy. I suggest that an intellectual environment that nourishes enquiry based upon intellectual love is one that is likely to evolve supportive interrelationships between teaching and research.

This concept of enquiry suggests that university teaching should take place in an environment that is enthused by research and also that university research should recognize its valuable contribution to teaching. This does not appear to be the case, in general, in the UK where research funding bodies make no requirement that research proposals should impact upon teaching. The situation is different in the USA, however, where the National Science Foundation (NSF) funds approximately 20 per cent of all federally supported basic research conducted by US colleges and universities (NSF 2005). Research proposals submitted to the NSF are required to indicate the contribution that the proposed research programme will make to teaching and this is an important criterion for funding.

Research funding arrangements in the UK, combined with the Research Assessment Exercise and government policies such as *The Future of Higher Education* (DfES 2003), have had the effect of increasing the tensions between teaching and research and undermining their symbiotic relationship. They have also tended to privilege institutions and the careers of individuals that have a strong research rather than teaching record. In response to this, the UK's Higher Education Academy (following its forerunner, the Institute for Learning and Teaching in Higher Education) has sought to raise the status of teaching.

The argument of this chapter is that rather than putting emphasis upon raising the status of teaching, institutions should be concerned to create the kinds of space in which research, as well as teaching, can be motivated by a love of knowledge. The qualities of such space are an increased acknowledgement of the values of risk, ignorance and trust and a reduced requirement for outcomes measurement, competition and predictability. Such a value position has immediate implications for how we work with colleagues. It will not ensure that good teachers become good researchers, or vice versa, but it will contribute to a culture in which research, teaching and learning can be mutually enhancing.

Far from being an outdated or 'medieval' basis for academic work, such an approach is important if teaching and research are to be innovatory, and are to address society's problems in the longer term, rather than merely respond to the rapidly changing fashions and funding streams of educational policy. It is also vital if the higher education system is to make the most of the enormous resource of academic staff who are driven by their love of their subject.

An implication of this argument for universities is that more attention should be given to the ways in which university structures (such as research institutes, teaching programmes and outreach activities) can draw teaching and research into closer relationships.

9
Conclusions

[F]ierce intellectual determination, as citizens, to define the real truth of our lives and our societies is a crucial obligation which devolves upon us all. It is in fact mandatory. If such a determination is not embodied in our political vision we have no hope of restoring what is so nearly lost to us – the dignity of man.

(Pinter 2005)

Introduction

I started this book with the words of a student who wanted to go to university to help make the world a better place. She knew, perhaps intuitively, that the intellectual project of a university education was also a moral project.

The playwright Harold Pinter (2005), in his Nobel Prize for Literature Lecture, graphically portrays a view of a world in which human dignity is threatened. In his above closing remarks he notes that its restoration requires 'intellectual determination'.

Ron Barnett opened his book *Higher Education: A Critical Business* (1997) with a picture and account of a student resisting the advance of a line of Chinese tanks in Tiananmen Square in 1989. The image depicts the student taking what Barnett calls a 'critical action', a characteristic of 'critical being'. Promoting critical being is, for Barnett, a defining aim of a higher education.

These three people, a student, playwright and academic, share the realization that intellectual and moral purposes are profoundly linked. This linkage has a solid tradition going back at least to Plato and his understanding of 'the good life'. It appears, however, to be threatened by a system of higher education in danger of losing its sense of intellectual, moral and social purposes. Higher education needs to write itself a new story based more closely upon intellectual and moral values connecting participants with the wider society. It will then be able to play its part in the determination 'to define the real truth of our lives and our societies', as Harold Pinter puts it.

In my attempts to contribute to such a new story I have developed a concept of the university's role as one of critical service, recognizing that at present the emphasis appears to be upon service, or rather servility, with little critique. Hope is nevertheless possible. Despite the increasing dominance of bureaucracy and managerialism, participants of the academic community are still motivated by educational values, albeit ones that go largely unrecognized in the accounts that higher education is required to give of itself. Fundamental to these is a conception of academic enquiry based upon the intellectual love that motivates learners, teachers and researchers.

Given that higher education is spoken of almost exclusively in the language of a market place, however, can this idea or ideal of the university based upon enquiry find expression? Can it even be understood by those who seem to be more inclined to view the search for truth as a relic of a bygone era? The difficulty here is of the same kind as that explored in the chapter on interdisciplinarity: it involves conflicting regimes of truth. The conclusion I drew about the story of Kennewick Man was not simply that the scientists and the American Indian community disagreed about what to do with the bones, but that they did not even share an understanding of the central concepts of the negotiation: 'populations' and 'peoples'. Similarly, the cultures of enquiry and management in universities seem unable to communicate with one another. It is difficult to envisage how Human Resources would speak of intellectual love.

But this is an oversimplification. The academic and managerial cultures in higher education are not mutually exclusive. Most university managers are still (or were once) academics and most academic staff, and arguably students, play a role in management. If the university consists of two cultures in conflict, it is a conflict that is to a large extent internalized by all involved. It is not so much a problem of 'us against them', but one of addressing the identity conflict that is experienced by all involved. Not so much how do *we* convince *you* of the importance of educational values, but how is one to deal with what Jack Whitehead (1993) calls 'the living contradiction' of attempting to live according to our educational values while also having to adopt the very different values of the institution?

Despite these difficulties, I hope to illustrate how the idea of enquiry, as I have elaborated it, might play a part in thinking through plans and strategies. In the process I will attempt to make some links between the terms I have used in the book and the terms in which higher education is more commonly addressed.

To do this, I will imagine a sympathetic yet critical reader who has taken the trouble to get to this final chapter, but still has questions hanging concerning the coherence of the ideas explored and their relevance to the experience of working in a university. The chapter then takes the form of an imagined conversation in which I address this reader's questions.

The conversation

You appear to object to the way universities are expected to give an account of themselves. But shouldn't I be expected to give an account of my teaching (or research, for that matter) in order to assure the student, tax payer or whoever that their money is well spent? And even if it is difficult, shouldn't we try to be objective about the way we measure performance? Are you really opposed to quality assurance, Stephen?

Yes, I'm quite happy to give an account of what I teach, how and why and to think about the results of my efforts. But let's be realistic. While it's relatively easy to provide certain objective measures, such as student pass rates, or satisfaction scores, the relationship between such measures and the value of my teaching is not at all clear. The things that really matter to me are not easily measurable. They are qualities rather than quantities – things like students' growing feeling for their subject, or their increasing ability to collaborate with their fellow students, or the extent to which they are able to make connections between the subject matter they are studying and their wider experience of life, or their particular insights or misunderstandings. Such things as these are important to note but not readily measured. Einstein is alleged to have said: 'Everything that's countable doesn't necessarily count; what counts isn't necessarily countable.' The danger with quality assurance is that it is inclined to give undue prominence to what is countable and thereby gives its judgements a spurious objectivity. The league table has become the dominant metaphor for making value judgements. Quality assurance seems to be more about quantity assurance. We are led to believe that 'quality indicators' identify items that can be counted to give a measure of quality. But even where the indicator is a reliable one, which it often isn't, we have the same problem as discussed in the last chapter in relation to research assessment: maximizing performance measures becomes the goal and quality teaching is reduced to game playing.

The teacher's instrumental concern to score well then readily transfers to the student who comes to see scoring well rather than a love of the subject as being what counts. The time teachers and students spend filling out feedback forms would be much better spent enquiring in some detail into specific instances that have a particular interest. For example, keeping reflective notes on how a new course is going, talking to students about their experience or building a detailed understanding of an individual's complex and unpredictable experience of learning reveals a great deal about the quality of educational engagement. Even the exchange of casual anecdotes about our students' or our own learning, with students as well as with other staff, can help learning to be viewed as an object of enquiry rather than audit. It is more important that teachers and students try to understand each other than measure each other. And the measuring so often gets in the way of the understanding.

Yes, I can understand that satisfaction scores don't tell us much, but at least they ensure that all students get to have some say, even if it is superficial. That must at least redress the power imbalance in favour of students and ensure that the student experience is taken seriously.

It should do, but I'm not convinced that most students regard giving feedback to their teachers as empowering. As I pointed out in Chapter 5, there is evidence to suggest they view giving ratings with as much cynicism as their teachers (Johnson 2000). It's significant that in the first national survey of student experience of higher education to be conducted in the UK, student unions in universities such as Oxford, Cambridge and Warwick decided not to contribute to the survey, believing that it would distract them from their work and be of limited use (French 2005). Although a survey with such a wide scope is not quite the same as providing feedback to an individual lecturer, this does suggest that students would rather be engaged in an academic community than be treated merely as its customers. The development of the collegial relationships involved in mutual enquiry – into the experience of learning as well as the subject matter itself – conflicts strongly with the idea of the student as a customer whose satisfaction is to be measured.

The teachers you discussed in Chapter 3 seemed to feel that more student-centred methods contributed to greater democracy in the lecture room. What other methods enhance the student's sense of control, or agency, in teaching and learning?

I think we should be wary of associating a particular teaching method or technology with more democratic social relations in teaching. The teachers I spoke to in Chapter 3 from South Africa and Russia were moving out of very authoritarian societies. For some of them, breaking away from a narrow lecture format may have symbolized a move away from authoritarianism in teaching. The same has been the case in the UK, but I'm not sure that the lecture is such a powerful symbol of the teacher's authority any longer here.

My argument in the last chapter about the importance of loving the subject as a basis for enquiry is not quite the same as saying that teaching should be more centred on the student. Democracy in learning may not just be about a balance of power between teachers and learners, but a sense of shared intellectual love and equality, as co-enquirers, before the subject matter.

Over the last ten years or so academic and educational development professionals have put an enormous emphasis on teaching processes. These are important: thinking about teaching methods is very valuable. But the danger is that the focus on generic approaches to teaching, and theories of learning, can lead to a separation of teaching method and subject matter. Academic or educational developers come to be seen as experts in how to teach but ignorant about what to teach. Elsewhere I described such developers as being 'like experts of love who have no lover; or professors who have nothing to profess' (Rowland *et al.* 1998: 135). This leads to an artificial split between content and process, like the fragmentation between teaching and research. In teaching, process and content (rather like form and content in art) are tightly intertwined. In the UK the Learning and Teaching Subject Networks may do something to bring content and method together, but it is still too early to say.

You haven't said much about e-learning. Doesn't that have enormous potential for giving students more responsibility for their learning and control over it? And isn't that likely to promote more effective learning?

We need to be careful of the concept of 'effectiveness' here. Teaching methods are effective only in relation to specific contexts which include subject matter and educational purposes. The danger with talk of 'effectiveness' is that it draws undue attention to the technical effects of knowledge transmission and skill development rather than to wider educational purposes. It is a one-dimensional concept. I find it more helpful to think in terms of the value of a particular method in a given context as this directs thinking towards the particular ways in which it might be of value and the particular values that might underlie such a judgement.

When it comes to new digital technologies, virtual learning environments or the net in general there appear to be two broad perspectives which each offer some insight. One way of thinking emphasizes the net and digital communication in terms of complex systems and the possibilities for emergence of new structures. From this perspective the technologies are not readily controlled or managed from above and so have enormous potential for giving users more control. An example of this was the mobilization of mass demonstrations around the world in 2003 against the American and British plans to invade Iraq, which was only possible through the emergence of linked cells in networked communication. A smaller-scale example was when a group of Masters students took the initiative, using their email group in ways that could not have been predicted or controlled, and totally redirected the module they were studying and its form of assessment (see Rowland 2000: 70–2). These are certainly productive instances of technology expanding the opportunities for users to exert control. The potential here for learners to take responsibility for their learning and engage with each other and with a wealth of material is enormous.

On the other hand, others such as Land and Bayne (2002) draw upon the ideas of Foucault (1979) to emphasize the ways in which new technologies such as virtual learning environments provide a context of surveillance. Every learning move of students and teachers is open to inspection and therefore the possibility of control. Even email communication is no longer private. In virtual learning environments the traditional boundaries between the private and the public are changed and this has profound implications for how we understand control and democratic relationships in teaching. At the same time, the expense of developing online curriculum materials can only be justified through wide-scale application. For such reasons, some researchers (such as Spencer 2005) claim that one influence of digital technologies has been to move control of the curriculum away from local teachers and students towards more remote managers and external bodies.

Perhaps teachers have not adopted new technologies as rapidly as they might have due to technophobia, conservatism or an unpreparedness to change. But many may have a more considered view which is suspicious of the advantages claimed for new technologies in some contexts. The uncritically positive value that is placed upon innovation and change in this area needs to be challenged.

In practice, I think students should have an influential role in planning and deciding how they are to use new technologies, rather than being simply plugged into systems. This can be difficult with sophisticated systems designed by technical specialists who often have little educational understanding and may be working from different educational assumptions. Where students are able to take a greater degree of control of how new technologies are used in their learning, by generating their own websites and even their own courses, this can be genuinely empowering. It can also add a new dimension to their enquiry. University students are often more technologically competent than their teachers. We should be making the most of their abilities.

Surely the ways in which new technologies provide almost instant access to masses of information can only be of positive value in providing a rich learning environment? I'm thinking here as much of its value in my own research as in my students' learning.

I'm continually amazed at the power of Google to help me identify references and other sources of information. But I am uneasy about this ease. I could have found some reference to support almost every claim and argument I made in this book, for example. After all, one rarely says anything completely new. But to do so would have lent the text a completely spurious authority.

The problem is that it is easy to mistake information for knowledge, or to replace argument by soundbite, or to suppose that an idea is valid (or of value) because it has been made public and can be found on the net. To draw upon the analogy of the last chapter, such use of technology can lead to intellectual promiscuity: 'easy come, easy go' encounters with information rather than engagement based upon intellectual love. The ease with which one can encounter almost any idea on the net makes it even more important to test its provenance. This is particularly difficult for students. It's another reason that I think it is important to give much more attention to the subject matter, the forms of argument and the kinds of knowledge claims that are made and the basis of their authority. Lists of references and quotations in student essays impress me much less than they used to.

On the other hand, the speed with which one can move from one form of knowledge and one frame of reference to another can lead to useful insights. It can certainly help in making the kinds of leaps over boundaries that is part of interdisciplinary work. For example, when I wrote the first draft that eventually became Chapter 2, I invented, or thought I had invented, the term 'critical servant' to indicate the university's relationship with society. I decided to put the phrase into Google to see if anyone else had used the term and discovered many references pointing to an Ancient Greek rhetorician called Isocrates. I had never heard of him, but it led me to a number of readings in both Classics and literary criticism about rhetorics, which were totally outside my disciplinary background. I make passing reference to this in Chapter 8 on enquiry. No doubt my understanding of the issues is still very shallow, but the connections were nevertheless very thought-provoking and helped develop my argument. But perhaps of more importance to me is that this has led me down an avenue of enquiry that I'm still investigating. Such use of technology is not predisposed towards bureaucracy, control and prescribed outcomes: more a spirit of adventure.

Thus the ease of access to new information can lead to superficiality, or it can lead to new ideas which may be only partly understood but nevertheless valuable in setting off new lines of enquiry. I think we have to be careful in our own research as well as with our students' learning. It is not always easy to distinguish real insight and understanding from superficiality. This applies equally in reviewing journal articles as in assessing students' coursework.

The current obsession with student plagiarism sometimes misses this point. The solution is not to search for more and more effective technical devices for outwitting the cheats and their accomplices, but to devise forms of assessment that really challenge students to express themselves, and their examiners to engage with them. That makes severe demands upon resources. Given the enormous potential of the internet, perhaps there needs to be much less assessment, but in ways that are more genuinely communicative. I think there is some hope here that the tide is turning against ever-increasing assessment, and making assessment more closely related to learning.

You speak a great deal of the need to avoid shallowness and be critical, especially in interdisciplinary research. But an individual can only do so much. If we're really to engage with others who come with different backgrounds, how can we respond to their ideas critically without undergoing the disciplined learning they've gone through? Aren't we just faced with a choice here: either to know a little in depth or a lot superficially, whether we are talking about the students' curriculum or academic research?

It sometimes seems like this; but I think the distinction often made between depth and breadth, whether applied to academic research or to student

124   *The Enquiring University*

learning, can be misconceived. Judgements about the depth and super-ficiality of someone's understanding are highly dependent upon context and purpose.

I am part of a large interdisciplinary research programme which involves taking part in seminars given by historians, lawyers, statisticians and others whose work is often unfamiliar to me (UCL 2003). I am at times only too aware of the superficiality of my own understanding of their disciplines. I have noticed that my response to this awareness tends to go through two phases. In the first phase I am inclined to reject their approach, their assumptions and their expertise as being irrelevant to my interests. I often feel this opposition to be about important and firmly held values. This can, however, be used as an excuse to avoid the difficulties of learning new material. In this phase I am inclined to defend my disciplinary territory against what may be seen as colonization by the other and to view the discipline of others in terms of stereotypes. Relationships in this phase can become quite embattled, often along the lines of the sciences versus the social sciences and humanities or upon ideological lines. It can even lead to the demise of interdisciplinary collaboration.

The second phase is more open. I now acknowledge my own ignorance and am prepared to listen and ask even when I feel confused. I take the risk of expressing the superficiality of my understanding, uncovering ignorance and trusting that others will not subject this to ridicule. It can be quite humbling but also enriching. My attitude is much more consistent with intellectual love. It involves a sense of awe in the enormous amount I have to learn and the limitations of my understanding. This is a good basis for research even if it feels risky and uncomfortable at times. It also engenders more support and collegiality and less disciplinary tribalism (Becher 1989).

I think there are aspects of academic culture that make this difficult: its competitiveness, its intolerance of uncertainty and its lack of humility. We have to be courageous to resist those cultural norms and values. While a depth (or should it be a height?) of understanding is something we are all aiming for, I'm wary of those who speak of 'academic rigour' as though that were a straightforward fixed concept. That is only so in a static system. Within dynamic disciplinary frameworks 'rigour' is always a contestable concept. That's not to say it's meaningless or unimportant, but claims about rigour need to be treated with caution. Often they have more to do with inflexibility and *rigor mortis* than with intellectual thoroughness. Again, it's a question of the tension between complying with the canons of disciplinary knowledge and also contesting them.

You talk a lot about values, particularly educational values. Professional bodies like the Higher Educational Academy also talk about professional values. Much of this talk I find just a matter of rhetoric: statements of the blindingly obvious with which one cannot disagree. Yet the basis of your argument appears to be that the values of enquiry should underpin all academic work. Some of these values, like intellectual love, you've talked about. But I'm still not sure what exactly you mean by a value?

You're right to challenge my use of that term. Talk about values can seem more appropriate to a sermon than to a thoughtful enquiry. Alternatively, we could get very philosophical in attempting to define values, and I don't want to do that here. Let me just suggest a simple strategy for illuminating a value position.

Ask someone why they do something. The question can be anything as big as 'why do you do research?' or as small as 'why did you mark that student's work with a red pen?' However the question is answered, simply ask why again in relation to that answer. Keep asking why until no further response can be given. The end point then illuminates a value position.

So, for example, imagine we are questioning a chemist who teaches first-year undergraduates about electrons and the Periodic Table. We want to understand why this is given as a lecture rather than, say, a handout or tutorial. The response might go like this:

> I give it as a lecture because this is a set of ideas they have to get right; they have to get it right because it's fundamental to inorganic chem-istry; it's fundamental because understanding the rest of the course depends upon it; they have to understand the course because otherwise they won't pass the exam; they have to pass the exam because they need the qualification; they need the qualification because that's why they came to university; because that's what university is for . . .

At this point the chemist finds it difficult to continue answering 'why?' We are now close to a value position which the lecturer holds concerning the role of the university as provider of qualifications.

In this example the response could, however, have followed a very different path such as this:

> I give it as a lecture because these ideas beautifully illustrate how chemists think; seeing me demonstrate how chemists think might inspire them to try to think that way; being inspired may motivate them to learn to think like chemists too; they need to think like chemists because they are to become participants in the discipline of chemistry; they need to participate in chemistry because they must participate in disciplinary knowledge; because that's what universities are for . . .

Again the lecturer finds it difficult to continue and we are now near to a value position which again concerns the purpose of the university. But this time its purpose is as a custodian of disciplinary knowledge rather than a provider of qualifications. A chain of thinking like this underlies Valenta's fine description of a lecture in a paper called 'To see a chemist thinking' (Valenta 1974). According to him, the main purpose of a lecture is to enable the student to engage with a particular way of thinking.

It is of course possible to value the university both as a custodian of disciplinary knowledge and as a qualifications provider. But the two values conflict. One cannot always avoid conflicts of value, but an awareness of such conflicts can be helpful, even in such a mundane task as planning a lecture. My expectation would be that a lecture given as an expression of the latter value position would be different from a lecture motivated by the former value: more concerned to portray a way of thinking than to communicate a body of knowledge.

You asked me what I mean by a value. In attempting to illustrate what a value might be I've also shown that a particular technique is not necessarily expressive of a particular value position. A lecture can be an expression of both value positions. This applies to 'innovations in teaching and learning' as much as it does to lecturing. That's why, in the last chapter, I didn't envisage intellectual love and the value of enquiry as an argument for or against lectures or any other methods, as such. It is rather an appeal to a value that should underlie choice and use of methods. But it can be difficult to maintain such a value in an environment of compliance.

You seem to have suggested that management is the problem here: that it is the culture of management that demands compliance and undermines any such value as intellectual love. But surely managers who are concerned to promote excellence are also trying to promote such educational values?

I wonder. I have just been considering a set of proposals from a Human Resources Department relating to the training programme for senior university managers. Amongst the competences that the programme aims to develop is 'the promotion of excellence'. Of course everyone wants to promote excellence although, like some of the examples in Chapter 4, the idea of this being a competence is rather strange. But I don't see how you could be against promoting excellence. The question at issue here, however, should be 'excellence in what?' The problem with the rhetoric of 'excellence', rather like the rhetoric of 'effectiveness' discussed above, is that it readily conceals questions about purposes. Purposes inevitably involve values which are subjective or relative in the sense that they are always contestable. The jargon of managerialism avoids questions of value in order to maintain objectivity and avoid contestation. But it is a spurious objectivity since it avoids the primary issue: the purposes of educational activity. A characteristic of managerialist discourse is its appearance of objectivity and freedom from values. It is on this basis of supposed objectivity that compliance is demanded. What remains hidden, however, are the particular ideological values that shape it.

But that is managerialism. Management can resist the ideology of managerialism. To do that it must propose an alternative set of values: it must put forward what Barnett (2003) calls an 'idealogy'. The values of enquiry, as I have explored them, express such an idealogy. Educational management based upon educational values is not managerialist. It seeks to develop collegiality, welcomes debate about purpose, seeks to explore values and acknowledge differences. It 'is about embracing the otherness of others' as one senior manager put it (Barton and Rowland 2003: 570). In fact, good management, like good teaching and good research, works creatively within the tension between compliance and contestation as it struggles to create a shared identity amongst diverse individuals. A principal of an institution, in the same interview, reflected upon this similarity between management and teaching: 'One of the reasons that I quite like being a manager is that I think management is as much a form of pedagogy, as pedagogy involves management. So I don't see in theory a sharp distinction [between teaching and management] ...' (Barton and Rowland 2003: 573).

In practice, however, it may be even more difficult for the manager than for the teacher to develop relationships that value critical engagement. As the same principal admitted:

> I think that the notion that there is full critical exchange between senior managers and universities and the members of the academy, is not only a bit of a myth now, but has always been a bit of a myth. I think probably we need a different model than either the one we have got now or the traditional one if management is to become a real learning activity.
>
> (Barton and Rowland 2003: 573)

An enquiring university strives towards management becoming 'a real learning activity'. It's not management *per se* that is the source of over-bearing compliance. It is the way of thinking about management that is inappropriate to enquiring institutions. If the concept of enquiry that I have explored in this book is significant in thinking about teaching and research, it is equally significant in thinking about university management. In Chapter 5 I suggested that a task of academic development should be to remind management of its educational values. This is not a rejection of management but a reminder that educational management should be educational rather than managerial. Inasmuch as all academic staff and students have to manage their educational activity, the reminder is for each. Each is responsible for the values that inform their activity.

You appear to be placing the responsibility for adopting a more enquiry-oriented approach to higher education squarely upon the shoulders of each member of staff. But doesn't such change have to be managed and organized by setting up structures, objectives, targets and all the rest? And then aren't we back again into managerialism? How is change to be managed? What about those who resist change?

Again, the way language is used here is a problem. There is nothing inherently good or bad about change or innovation. Enquiry involves being prepared to try out new things, take risks and accept uncertainty. But it does not follow that the new way is better. The 'fierce intellectual determination' that Harold Pinter speaks of above is as much an imperative to resist falsehood as it is to change for the better. In fact his lecture was very much concerned with resisting the falsehoods of the politically powerful. The idea of resistance as a positive expression of educational value, however, does not sit comfortably with the idea of change management in higher education. I think that in our concern to promote the value of enquiry we need to be much more forceful, thoughtful and articulate about resisting the influences that oppose it.

The idea of resistance has, at different times and places (such as in Tiananmen Square in 1989), been associated with radical, progressive, enlightened action; in higher education it is often now associated with conservatism and elitism. In the present situation it is particularly important to articulate what resistance is for rather than merely what it is against. It is easy, for example, to fudge and play lip service to inappropriate practices of audit, or to bury one's head in the sand; it is much more difficult and dangerous to respond articulately, explaining the importance of promoting the academic values of enquiry rather than simply objecting to bureaucracy.

I have often attended committee meetings where a decision is about to be made that clearly conflicts with the values of enquiry. Often I do not have the courage to raise my voice, or think there is little I can do, or feel that the only way to express a view is in a language that is very different from the language of the committee. But at others I speak up and am surprised to find that, once the ice has been broken, others too are prepared to express a more enlightened view. Management is as much about managing these small moments as it is about managing larger structures. And it is in such moments that change can be conceived.

So is that why you are hopeful? Is it in the small ways in which each of us can make a difference?

Yes it is. But let's not be naive about this. My observation is that there is an enormous intellectual resource amongst staff, students and others who work with higher education. The survey that found most staff considered academic life stressful but found many aspects of their work rewarding (see page 60) seems to confirm this observation. Academic life and the opportunity for enquiry is still enjoyed and appreciated as a privilege by most. We can build on that. But we have to be imaginative and work to create the spaces – often very small spaces – for such conversation. We may then discover our shared interest in the kind of enquiring university that might contribute to making the world a better place.

References

Adonis, A. (1998) A Class Act. London: Penguin.

AHRC (Arts and Humanities Research Council) (2004) *AHRB News and Press Releases*, 15 October.

Allen, M. (1993) *A Conceptual Model of Transferable Personal Skills*. Sheffield: Employment Department.

Amarglio, J., Resnick, S. and Wolff, R. (1993) Division and difference in the 'discipline' of economics, in E. Messer-Davidow, D. Shumay and D. Sylvan, *Knowledges: Historical and Critical Studies in Disciplinarity*. Charlottesville, VA: University Press of Virginia.

Andresen, L. (1996) The work of academic development – occupational identity, standards of practice, and the virtues of association, *International Journal of Academic Development*, 1(1): 38–49.

Annan, N. (1999) *The Dons: Mentors, Eccentrics and Geniuses*. London: HarperCollins.

Armstrong, M. (1980) *Closely Observed Children: The Diary of a Primary School Classroom*. London: Writers & Readers.

AUT (Association of University Teachers) (2003) Privatisation plans attacked, *AUTlook*, January. London: Association of University Teachers.

Barnett, R. (1997) *Higher Education: A Critical Business*. Buckingham: Society for Research into Higher Education and Open University Press.

Barnett, R. (2000) *Realizing the University in an Age of Supercomplexity*. Buckingham: Society for Research in Higher Education and Open University Press.

Barnett, R. (2003) *Beyond All Reason: Living with Ideology in the University*. Buckingham: Society for Research into Higher Education and Open University Press.

Barnett, R. and Coate, K. (2005) *Engaging the Curriculum in Higher Education*. Maidenhead: McGraw-Hill.

Barthes, R. (1977) *Image – Music – Text*, trans. S. Heath. Glasgow: Fontana/Collins.

Barton, L. and Rowland, S. (2003) An interview with G. Whitty and M. Worton, *Teaching in Higher Education*, 8(4): 563–78.

Bath, D. and Smith, C. (2004) Academic developers: an academic tribe claiming their territory in higher education, *International Journal for Academic Development*, 9(1): 9–27.

BBSRC (Biotechnology and Biological Sciences Research Council) (2001) *Joint Statement of the Research Councils'/AHRB's Skills Training Requirements for Research Students*. Swindon: BBSRC.

Becher, T. (1989) *Academic Tribes and Territories*. Buckingham: Society for Research into Higher Education and Open University Press.

Bentham, J. (1810) *An Introductory View of the Rationale of Evidence for the Use of Non-Lawyers as well as Lawyers*, ed. James Mill 1809–11, first published in *Works*, vi, pp. 1–188, quoted in Twining (2003).

Berman M. (1982) *All That Is Solid Melts Into Air: The Experience of Modernity*. New York: Penguin.

Bhambra, M. (2005) *Professionalism in the Academic Community*. Unpublished Masters portfolio, University College London.

Blackstone, T. (2001) Why learn? Higher education in a learning society, *Higher Education Quarterly*, 55(2): 175–84.

Blake, N., Smith, R. and Standish, P. (1998) *The Universities We Need: Higher Education after Dearing*. London: Kogan Page.

Bleakley, A. (2001) From lifelong learning to lifelong teaching: teaching as a call to style, *Teaching in Higher Education*, 6(1): 113–17.

Blumenthal, L. (2005) Debate over Kennewick Man's remains now with lawmakers, *Tri-City Herald*, 1 February: 1.

Bok, D. (2003) *Universities in the Marketplace: The Commercialization of Higher Education*. Princeton, NJ and Oxford: Princeton University Press.

Bolton, G. (2003) Medicine, the arts, and the humanities, *The Lancet*, 362, 12 July: 93–4.

Booth, C. (1998) *Accreditation and Teaching in Higher Education*. London: Committee of Vice-Chancellors and Principals of the Universities of the United Kingdom.

Bourdieu, P. (1988) *Homo Academicus*. Oxford: Basil Blackwell.

Boyer, E. (1990) *Scholarship Reconsidered: Priorities of the Professoriate*. New York: HarperCollins.

Brew, A. (2001) *The Nature of Research: Inquiry in Academic Contexts*. London: Routledge Falmer.

Brew, A. and Boud, D. (1995) Teaching and research: stabilising the vital link with learning, *Higher Education*, 29: 261–73.

Bridges, D. (1992) Enterprise and liberal education, *Journal of Philosophy of Education*, 26(1): 91–8.

Broers, A. (2005) *The Triumph of Technology*. British Broadcasting Corporation (BBC) Reith Lectures, London, 6 April – 4 May.

Brown, M. and Precious, N. (1968) *The Integrated Day in the Primary Classroom*. London: Ward Lock.

Brown, R. (2005) *Higher Education: More than a Degree*. Summary of a consultation held at St George's House, Windsor Castle, 19–20 January. London: Council for Industry and Higher Education.

Browne, M. and Freeman, K. (2000) Distinguishing features of critical thinking classrooms, *Teaching in Higher Education*, 5(3): 301–9.

Bruner, J. (1966) *Toward a Theory of Instruction*. Cambridge, MA: Harvard University Press.

CACE (Central Advisory Council for Education) (England) (1967), *Children and their Primary Schools* (Plowden Report), Vol. 1. London: HMSO.

CAGS (Canadian Association for Graduate Studies) (2005) Programme for the conference: Challenges to Innovation in Graduate Education, Toronto, 2–5 December.

Calman, K. (2000) *A Study of Story Telling, Humour and Learning in Medicine*. London: Nuffield Trust.

Carnoy, M. and Levin, H. (1985) *Schooling and Work in the Democratic State*. Stanford, CA: Stanford University Press.

Carr, W. and Kemmis, S. (1986) *Becoming Critical: Education, Knowledge and Action Research*. Lewes: Falmer Press.

Carrotte, P. (1994) An action research cycle in the teaching of restorative dentistry: how my students respond to an invitation to take control and involvement in their own learning. Unpublished MEd dissertation, University of Sheffield.

Charlton, B. (1999) QAA: Why we should not collaborate, *Oxford Magazine*, 169: 8–10.

CHE (Committee on Higher Education) (1963) *Higher Education: Report of the Committee Appointed by the Prime Minister under the Chairmanship of Lord Robbins*, 1961–63, Cm 2154. London: HMSO.

Chomsky, N. (1983) Interview (with Noam Chomsky), *Omni*, 6 (2): November.

CIHE (Council for Industry and Higher Education) (2003) *Ethics and the Role of Higher Education*. London: Council for Industry and Higher Education.

Clark, B. (2000) Collegial entrepreneurialism in proactive universities: lessons from Europe, *Change*, January/February: 10–19.

Clark, N. (1996) The critical servant: an Isocratean contribution to critical rhetoric, *Quarterly Journal of Speech*, 82: 111–24.

Clarke, C. (2003) Letter to the *Times Higher Education Supplement*, 12 May: 19.

Coffield, F. (1999) Breaking the consensus: lifelong learning as social control, Inaugural Lecture, University of Newcastle, 2 February.

Cowell, R. (1995) Foreword to P. Carrotte and M. Hammond (eds) *Teaching and Learning in Difficult Times*. Sheffield: UK Universities' and Colleges' Staff Development Agency.

Davidson, M. (2004) Bones of contention: using self and story in the quest to professionalize higher education teaching – an interdisciplinary approach, *Teaching in Higher Education*, 9(3): 299–310.

Dawkins, R. (1998) *Unweaving the Rainbow: Science, Delusion and the Appetite for Wonder*. London: Penguin.

Dearden, R. (1968) *The Philosophy of Primary Education*. London: Routledge & Kegan Paul.

de Bono, E. (1982) *de Bono's Thinking Course*. London: British Broadcasting Corporation.

de Botton, A. (2001) *The Consolations of Philosophy*. London: Penguin.

DE (Department of Education) (1988) *Education Reform Act*. London: HMSO.

Derrida, J. (1996) *Archive Fever: A Freudian Impression*, trans. E. Prenowitz. Chicago, IL: University of Chicago Press.

Detrez, C. and Grossetti, M. (1998) How to import a science: the beginning of chemical engineering in France, paper presented to the European Association for the Study of Science and Technology Congress, Lisbon, 30 September–4 October.

Devine, M., Mingard, S., Fenwick, N. and Black, H. (1994) *School for Skills*. Edinburgh: Scottish Council for Research in Education.

Dewey, J. (1939) *Freedom and Culture*. New York: Putman.

Dewey, J. (1941) *Education Today*. London: George Allen & Unwin.

DfEE (Department for Education and Employment) (1996) *Literature Review of the Impact of the Work-Related Curriculum on 14–16 Year Olds*, RS 33. London: HMSO.

DfES (Department for Education and Skills) (2003) *The Future of Higher Education*, Cm 5735. London: HMSO.

132   *References*

Diogenes Laërtius (1895) *The Lives and Opinions of Eminent Philosophers: Book VII: The Stoics*, trans. C.D. Yonge. London: George Bell & Sons.

Eco, U. (1987) *Travels in Hyperreality*. London: Picador.

ED (Employment Department) 1989 *Key Features of the Enterprise in Higher Education Proposals*. Sheffield: Training Agency.

Egan, T. (1999) Expert panel recasts origin of fossil man in northwest, *New York Times*, 16 October: 10.

Elton, L. (2001) Research and teaching: what are the real relationships?, *Teaching in Higher Education*, 6(1): 43–56.

Elwes, R. (1955) (trans.) *The Chief Works of Benedict de Spinoza. The Ethics*. New York: Dover.

Entwistle, N. (1992) *The Impact of Teaching on Learning Outcomes in Higher Education*. Sheffield: Committee of Vice-Chancellors and Principals.

Eraut, M. (1994) *Developing Professional Knowledge and Competence*. London: Falmer Press.

Evans, G. (2002) *Academics and the Real World*. Buckingham: Society for Research into Higher Education and Open University Press.

Evans, M. and Greaves, D. (1999) Exploring the medical humanities, *British Medical Journal*, 319: 1216.

Evans, M. and Macnaughton, J. (2004) Should medical humanities be a multi-disciplinary or an interdisciplinary study?, *Medical Humanities*, 30: 1–4.

Feller, I. (2005) Beyond initiatives: the problematic institutionalization of inter-disciplinary graduate degree programs in American research universities, paper presented to the 2005 international conference: Challenges in Innovation in Graduate Education, Toronto, 2–5 November.

Feyerabend, P. (1975) *Against Method: Outline of an Anarchistic Theory of Knowledge*. London: New Left Books.

Foucault, M. (1979). *Discipline and Punish: The Birth of the Prison*. Harmondsworth: Penguin.

Fraser, K. (1999) Australasian academic developers: entry into the profession and our own professional development, *International Journal of Academic Development*, 4(2): 89–101.

Fraser, K. (2001) Australasian academic developers' conceptions of their profession, *International Journal of Academic Development*, 6(1): 54–64.

Freire, P. (1972) *Pedagogy of the Oppressed*. London: Penguin.

French, D. (2005) Undergraduate survey riles unions, *Times Higher Education Supplement*, 25 March: 1.

Friedman, T.L. (2000) *The Lexus and the Olive Tree: Understanding Globalization*. New York: Anchor Books.

Furedi, F. (2004) *Where Have All the Intellectuals Gone?* London: Continuum.

Geuna, A. and Martin, B. (2001) *University Research Evaluation and Funding: An International Comparison*. Science and Technology Policy Research Paper No. 71. Brighton: University of Sussex.

Gibbons, M., Limoges, C., Nowotny, H., Schwartzman, S., Scott, P. and Trow, M. (1994) *The New Production of Knowledge*. London: Sage Publications.

Glaser, R. and Chi, M.T.H. (1988) Overview, in M.T.H. Chi, R. Glaser and M. Farr (eds) *The Nature of Expertise*. Hillsdale, NJ: Erlbaum.

Gleick, J. (1988) *Chaos*. London: Heinemann.

Gleick, J. (2003) *Isaac Newton*. London: Pantheon Books.

Goodhart, C. (1984) *Monetary Theory and Practice*. London: Macmillan.

Gosling, D. (1997) Educational development and institutional change in higher education, in K. Moti Gokulsing and C. DaCosta (eds) *Usable Knowledges as the Goal of University Education*. London: Edwin Mellen Press.

Gould, E. (2003) *The University in a Corporate Culture*. New Haven, CT and London: Yale University Press.

Green, B. and Bigum, C. (1990) Quantum curriculum and chaotic classrooms: re-framing educational computing, in A. McDougall and C. Dowling (eds) *Computers in Education*. North-Holland: Elsevier Science.

Grossetti, M. (2005) Interdisciplinarity or hybrid disciplines: the example of 'sciences for the engineer' in France, paper presented to the 2005 international conference: Challenges in Innovation in Graduate Education, Toronto, 2–5 November.

Grundy, S. (1992) Beyond guaranteed outcomes: creating a discourse for educational praxis, *Australian Journal of Education*, 36(2): 157–69.

Halsey, A., Floud, J. and Anderson, C. (1961) *Education, Economy and Society: A Reader in the Sociology of Education*. New York: Free Press.

Hattie, J. and Marsh, H. (1996) The relationship between research and teaching: a meta-analysis, *Review of Educational Research*, 66(4): 507–42.

Havel, V. (1990) *Disturbing the Peace: A Conversation with Karel Hvizdala*, trans. Paul Wilson. New York: Vintage Books.

HEA (Higher Education Academy) (2004) *Guidance Notes for Referees on Supporting an Application to Join the HEA*. York: Higher Education Academy.

HEA (2005) *Strategic Plan 2005–2010*. York: Higher Education Academy.

HEFCE (Higher Education Funding Council) (2000) *HEFCE Review of Research: Consultation Document 00/37*. London: HEFCE.

HEFCE (2003) *Improving Standards in Postgraduate Research Degree Programmes*. London: HEFCE.

HEFCE (2004) Funding method for teaching from 2004–05. London: HEFCE.

Heidegger, M. (1977) Science and reflection, in *The Question Concerning Technology and Other Essays*, trans. W. Lovitt. New York: Harper & Row.

Heintz, J. and Folbre, N. (2000) *Field Guide to the US Economy*. New York: New Press.

Hennessy, J. (2002) Going forward: the challenges ahead after a year of change, *Stanford Report*, 19 April. http://news-service.stanford.edu/news/2002/april24/acadcounciltext.html (accessed 11 May 2006).

Hertz, N. (2001) *The Silent Takeover: Global Capitalism and the Death of Democracy*. London: Heinemann.

Hodge, M. (2001) (Interviewed by A. Goddard) Hodge puts her weight behind QAA, *Times Higher Educational Supplement*, 15 June: 1.

Holmes, L. (1998) One more time, transferable skills don't exist ... (and what we should do about it), paper presented to the conference: Higher Education for Capability, Nene College, Northampton, 27 February.

Horkheimer, M. (1972) *Critical Theory: Selected Essays*, trans. Matthew J. O'Connell and others. Toronto: Herder & Herder.

Huang, C. (1997) *The Analects of Confucius (Lun Yu). A Literal Translation with an Introduction and Notes*. Oxford: Oxford University Press.

Irvine, D. (2001) Speech to the Royal Society of Medicine, *Independent*, 16 January: 1.

Jenkins, A. (1996) Discipline-based educational development, *International Journal for Academic Development*, 1(1): 50–62.

Johnson, R. (2000) The authority of the student evaluation questionnaire, *Teaching in Higher Education*, 5(4): 419–34.

Kinman, G. and Jones, F. (2004) *Working to the Limit: Stress and Work–Life Balance in*

Academic and Academic-Related Employees in the UK. London: Association of University Teachers.

Klein, N. (2001) *No Logo.* London: HarperCollins.

Kroker, A. (1980) Migration from the disciplines, *Journal of Canadian Studies,* 15(3): 3–10.

Kushner, S. (2004) Democracy – the unfinished revolution, paper presented to ESRC Seminar Series: Democracy, Education and Methodology, University of the West of England, Bristol, 26–7 February.

Land, R. (2001) Agency, context and change in academic development, *International Journal of Academic Development,* 6(1): 4–20.

Land, R. and Bayne, S. (2002) Screen or monitor? Surveillance and disciplinary power in online learning environments, in C. Rust (ed.) *Improving Student Learning through Learning Technology.* Oxford: Oxford Centre for Staff and Learning Development.

Lave, J. and Wenger, E. (1999) Learning and pedagogy in communities of practice, in J. Leach and B. Moon (eds) *Learners and Pedagogy.* Milton Keynes: Paul Chapman/Open University Press.

Learning and Skills Council (2003) *Plan Led Funding for FE,* Circular 03/15. London: Learning and Skills Council.

Lee, M. (1999) New World habitation tricky issue, *Kennewick Man Virtual Interpretive Center.* Washington, DC: Tri-City Herald, 26 December.

Leftwich, A. (1991) Pedagogy for the depressed: the political economy of teaching development in British universities, *Studies in Higher Education,* 16(3): 277–90.

Lenoir, T. (1993) The discipline of nature and the nature of disciplines, E. Messer-Davidow, D. Shumay and D. Sylvan, *Knowledges: Historical and Critical Studies in Disciplinarity.* Charlottesville, VA: University Press of Virginia.

Levacic, R. (1993) Education, in R. Maidment and G. Thompson (eds) *Managing the United Kingdom.* London: Sage Publications.

Levin, H. (1999) What is clearing technology? *Free Spirit Journal: Journal of Modern Techniques for Spiritual Development,* XVI (1 and 2): 35–9.

Lightfoot, L. (2004) How plagiarism on the internet has become part of the campus culture, *Daily Telegraph,* 27 July.

Lipsett, A. (2004) Staff claim UCL shake-up 'downgrades' academics, *Times Higher Educational Supplement,* 5 November: 56.

Louth, A. (2003) The unholy market kills divine life of the mind, *Times Higher Education Supplement,* 19 May: 18–19.

LSE (London School of Economics) (2003) The nature of evidence: how well do 'facts' travel? Research project funded by Leverhulme Trust and Economic and Social Research Council.

Luby, A. (1995) An enterprising approach to democratising the curriculum: reflections on a Scottish experience, *Journal of Vocational Education and Training,* 47(1): 21–33.

Lyotard, J-F. (1984) *The Postmodern Condition: A Report on Knowledge,* trans. G. Bennington and B. Masumi. Minneapolis, MN: University of Minnesota Press.

Macfarlane, B. (2003) *Teaching with Integrity –The Ethics of Higher Education Practice.* Basingstoke: Taylor & Francis.

McIntyre, M. (2001) *Audit, Education, and Goodhart's Law. Or, Taking Rigidity Seriously.* http://www.atm.damtp.cam.ac.uk/people/mem/papers/LHCE/dilnot-analysis.html (accessed 23 July 2004).

McNay, I. (1998) The paradoxes of research assessment and funding, in M.H. Little and B. Little (eds) *Changing Relationships between Higher Education and the State.* London: Jessica Kingsley.

Malcolm, J. and Zukas, M. (2001) Bridging pedagogical gaps: conceptual discontinuities in higher education, *Teaching in Higher Education*, 6(1): 33–42.

Marton, F., Beaty, E. and Dall'Alba, G. (1993) Conceptions of learning, *International Journal of Educational Research*, 19: 277–300.

Marton, F., Hounsell, D.J. and Entwistle, N.J. (1997) (eds) *The Experience of Learning* (2nd edition). Edinburgh: Scottish Academic Press.

Marx, K. and Engels, F. (1969) *Marx/Engels Selected Works, Volume One.* Moscow: Progress Publishers, pp. 98–137, checked and corrected against the English edition of 1888, by A. Blunden, 2004.

Maskell, D. and Robinson, I. (2001) *The New Idea of a University.* London: Haven Books.

Meek, J. (2001) Why the management style of a Danish hearing-aid maker may hold the key to stopping Bin Laden, *Guardian*, 18 October, G2: 2–3.

Messer-Davidow, E. (ed.) (1993) *Knowledges: Historical and Critical Studies in Disciplinarity.* Charlottesville, VA: University of Virginia.

Metcalfe, J., Thompson, Q. and Green, H. (2002) *Improving Standards in Postgraduate Research Degree Programmes. A Report to the Higher Education Funding Councils of England, Scotland and Wales.* London: Council for Graduate Education.

Miller Smith, C. (2002) A business view of the graduate today, *Exchange*, 2: 8–11, quoted in Barnett and Coate (2005).

Montaigne, M. de (1935) *The Essays of Montaigne*, trans. E.J. Trechman. London: Oxford University Press.

Mueller, M. (1989) Yellow stripes and dead armadillos: some thoughts on the current state of English studies, *Association of Departments of English Bulletin*, 92: 5–12, reprinted in *Profession 89*, New York: MLA, 23–31.

NAPAG (National Academies Policy Advisory Group) (1996) *Research Capability of the University System.* London: Royal Society.

National Academies (2005) *Facilitating Interdisciplinary Research.* Washington, DC: National Academies Press.

NCIHE (National Committee of Enquiry Into Higher Education) (1997) *Higher Education and the Learning Society* (the Dearing Report). London: HMSO.

NERF (National Educational Research Forum) (2000) *Research and Development for Education: A National Strategy Consultation Paper.* Nottingham: NERF Publications.

Nixon, J., Marks, A., Rowland, S. and Walker, M. (2001) Towards a new academic professionalism: a manifesto for hope, *British Journal of Sociology of Education*, 22(2): 227–44.

NSF (National Science Foundation) (2005) *About the National Science Foundation.* http://www.nsf.gov/about/ (accessed 30 November 2005)

OECD (Organization for Economic Co-operation and Development) (1998) *Review of National Policies for Education: Russian Federation.* Paris: OECD Centre for Cooperation with Non-members.

O'Neill, O. (2002) *A Question of Trust.* The BBC Reith Lectures. Cambridge: Cambridge University Press.

Panayotidis, E. (2001) Paradigms lost and paradigms gained: negotiating interdisciplinarity in the twenty-first century, *Border Crossing*, Fall, University of Calgary.

Parker, D. and Stacey, R. (1994) *Chaos, Management and Economics: The Implications of Non-Linear Thinking.* London: Institute of Economic Affairs.

Pilger, J. (2002) *The New Rulers of the World*. London: Verso.

Pinter, H. (2005) Art, truth and politics, Nobel Lecture, 7 December. Stockholm: The Nobel Foundation.

Popper, K. (1979) *Objective Knowledge: An Evolutionary Approach* (Revised edition). Oxford: Oxford University Press.

Prigogine, I. and Stengers, I. (1985) *Order out of Chaos*. London: Fontana.

Proust, M. (1934) *Remembrance of Things Past*. New York: Random House.

Pryse, M. (1998) Critical interdisciplinarity, women's studies, and cross-cultural insight, *National Women's Studies Association Journal*, 10(1): 1–22.

QAAHE (Quality Assurance Agency for Higher Education) (2004) *Code of Practice for the Assurance of Academic Quality and Standards in Higher Education. Section 1: Postgraduate Research Programmes*. Gloucester: QAAHE.

Qamar uz Zaman (2004) *Review of the Academic Evidence of the Relationship between Teaching and Research in Higher Education*, RR 506. London: DfES.

Radley, A. (1980) Student learning as social practice, in P. Salmon (ed.) *Coming to Know*. London: Routledge & Kegan Paul.

Radnedge, A. (2005) Work experience girl saves firm £250,000, *Metro*, 24 May: 9.

Raffle, J. (2005) Review of Lord Broers' third Reith lecture, 'Management and innovation', recorded in Manchester and broadcast 20 April 2005. Manchester Technology Fund, http://www.mantechfund.com/reith-lecture-print.htm, (accessed 10 Nov 2005).

Readings, B (1996) *The University in Ruins*. Cambridge, MA: Harvard University Press.

Reich, R. (2004) The destruction of public higher education in America, and how the UK can avoid the same fate, paper presented to the Higher Education Policy Institute Annual Lecture, London, 24 March.

Roberts, G. (2002) *Set for Success. The Report of Sir Gareth Roberts' Review*. London: HM Treasury.

Robertson, J. (1935) Introduction, in M. De Montaigne, *The Essays of Montaigne*, trans. E.J. Trechman. London: Oxford University Press, xi–xlx.

Rogers, C. (1969) *Freedom to Learn: A View of What Education Might Become*. Columbus: Charles E. Merrill.

Rogers, C. (1978) *Rogers on Personal Power*. London: Constable.

Rorty, R. (1982) *Contingency, Irony, Solidarity*. Cambridge: Cambridge University Press.

Rowland, S. (1984) *The Enquiring Classroom*. Lewes: Falmer Press.

Rowland, S. (1993) *The Enquiring Tutor*. Lewes: Falmer Press.

Rowland, S. (1996) Relationships between teaching and research, *Teaching in Higher Education*, 1(1): 7–20.

Rowland, S. (2000) *The Enquiring University Teacher*. Buckingham: Society for Research into Higher Education and Open University Press.

Rowland, S. (2001) Teaching for democracy in higher education. Paper presented to the Conference: Higher Education Close-Up, University of Lancaster, 16–18 July.

Rowland, S. (2002a) Overcoming fragmentation in professional life: the challenge for academic development, *Higher Education Quarterly*, 56(1): 52–64.

Rowland, S. (2002b) Interdisciplinarity as a site of contestation, paper presented to the annual conference of the British Education Research Association, University of Exeter, 12–14 September.

Rowland, S. and Barton, L. (1994) Making things difficult: developing a research approach to teaching in higher education, *Studies in Higher Education*, 19(3): 367–74.

Rowland, S., Byron, C., Furedi, F., Padfield, N. and Smyth, T. (1998) Turning academics into teachers?, *Teaching in Higher Education*, 3(2): 133–42.

Ryle, G. (1949) *The Concept of Mind*. London: Hutchinson.

Salvaggio, R. (1992) Women's studies and crossing (out) the disciplines, paper presented to the annual meeting of the Modern Language Association, New York, December.

Schuller, T. (1995) *The Changing University?*, Buckingham: Society for Research into Higher Education and Open University Press.

Schum, D. (2001) *Evidential Foundations of Probabilistic Reasoning*. Chichester: Wiley.

Schum, D. (2003) Evidence and inferences about past events, in W. Twining and I. Hampsher-Monk (eds) *Evidence and Inference in History and Law*. Evanston, IL: Northwestern University Press.

SIGN (Scottish Intercollegiate Guidelines Network) (2002) *Management of Patients with Stroke. Guideline 64*, November. Edinburgh: SIGN.

Smith, D. (2001) Collaborative research: policy and the management of knowledge creation in UK universities, *Higher Education Quarterly*, (55) 2: 131–57.

Snow, C.P. (1959) *The Two Cultures and the Scientific Revolution*. London: Cambridge University Press.

Sokal, A. and Bricmont, J. (1998) *Intellectual Impostures: Postmodern Philosophers' Abuse of Science*. London: Profile Books.

South Africa (1996) *National Education Policy Act*. Pretoria: Government Printer.

Spencer, H. (2005) Educational technology and issues of power and trust: barriers to the use of technology due to concerns over knowledge ownership, surveillance and power balance shifts, paper presented to the conference: Human Centred Technology, University of Sussex, 28–9 June.

Spinoza, B. (1992) *The Ethics. Treatise on the Emendation of the Intellect*, trans. S. Shirley. Indianapolis, IN: Hackett Publishing Company.

Squires, G. (1987) The curriculum, in T. Becher (ed.) *British Higher Education*. London: Allen & Unwin.

Stenhouse, L. (1975) *An Introduction to Curriculum Research and Development*. London: Heinemann.

Stenhouse, L. (1980) The study of samples and the study of cases, *British Educational Research Journal*, 6(1): 1–6.

Struppa, D. (2002) The nature of interdisciplinarity, *Journal of the Association of General and Liberal Studies*, 30(1): 97–105.

Szego, J. (2003) Shock finding on uni cheating, *The Age* (online journal) http://www.theage.com.au/articles/2003/01/06/1041566360939.html (accessed 27 July 2004).

Tagg, P. (2002) Conscientious objections to audit: background document to proposal submitted to the Association of University Teachers (AUT), February, http://www.mediamusicstudies.net/tagg/rants/audititis/autprop1.html (accessed 23 July 2004).

THES (Times Higher Education Supplement) (2003) Best gobbledegook of the year, *Times Higher Education Supplement*, 19/26, December: 20.

THES (2004) Global market set to shake up old rules, *Times Higher Education Supplement*, 11 June, Trends: iv.

Twining, W. (2003) Evidence as a multi-disciplinary subject, *Law, Probability and Risk*, 2: 91–107.

Tysome, T. (2003) Let's junk baffling jargon, says new LSC boss, *Times Higher Education Supplement*, 21 November: 11.

UCL (University College London) (2003) Evidence, inference and enquiry: towards an integrated science of evidence. Research project funded by Leverhulme Trust and Economic and Social Research Council.

UCL (University College London) (2004) Poster: 'Fulfilling the Promise', an advertisement for Advancing London's Global University – The Campaign for UCL. London: University College London.

Valenta, Z. (1974) To see a chemist thinking, in E. Sheffield (ed.) *Teaching in the Universities: No One Way.* Montreal: McGill/Queen's University Press.

Warhurst, C. (2001) Using debates in developing students' critical thinking, in M. Walker (ed.) *Reconstructing Professionalism in University Teaching.* Buckingham: Society for Research into Higher Education and Open University Press.

Whitehead, A. (1929) *The Aims of Education.* New York: Mentor Books.

Whitehead, J. (1993) *The Growth of Educational Knowledge: Creating Your Own Living Educational Theories.* Bournemouth: Hyde Publications.

Wilford, J. (1999) Archaeology and ancestry clash over skeleton, *New York Times,* 9 November: 4.

Winter, R. (1996) New liberty, new discipline, in R. Cuthbert (ed.) *Working in Higher Education.* Buckingham: Society for Research into Higher Education and Open University Press.

Wittgenstein, W. (1958) *The Blue and Brown Books: Preliminary Studies for the 'Philosophical Investigations'.* Oxford: Blackwell.

World Development Movement (2001) *Isn't It Time We Tackled the Causes of Poverty?* London: World Development Movement.

Yeats, W.B. ([1920] 1970) The second coming, in *Michael Robartes and the Dancer.* Shannon: Irish University Press.

Yeomans, D. (1996) *Constructing Vocational Education: From TVEI to GNVQ.* Paper No.1 of the Leeds University Post 14 Research Group. Leeds: Leeds University.

Yorke, M. (2004) Institutional research and higher education performance, *Journal of Higher Education Policy and Management,* 26(2): 141–52.

Index

Global citizenship 63
Globalization 12, 15, 20, 28, 34, 36 *see also* Market
Goodhart, C. 114
Gosling, D. 83
Greaves, D. 101
Green, B. 2
Grosetti, M. 90, 94, 101
Halsey, A. 113
Hattie, J. 6, 112
Havel, V. 14
Heidegger, M. 91
Heintz, J. 15
Hennessy, J. 97
Hertz, N. 15
Higher Education Academy (HEA) 44, 69, 115, 124
Higher Education Funding Council for England (HEFCE) 6, 10, 49
Higher education studies 12, 74, 83–5
Hodge, M. 20
Holmes, L. 53
Hope 2, 3, 10, 27, 128
Horkheimer, M. 93
Huang 14
Idealism 1, 2
Identity *see* Disciplinarity, identity; Academic development, identity
Individualism 42, 113
Institute of Learning and Teaching in Higher Education 69
Intellectual love 2, 13, 26, 109–116
Interdisciplinarity
  collaboration 100
  conditions for 101–2
  constraints upon 97
  critical 70–1, 78–9, 81, 92–3, 102
  in journals 98
  in research 94–5, 97–100, 124
  see also Academic development, critical interdisciplinary approach to; Disciplinarity, differences; Multidisciplinarity; Transdisciplinarity
International Journal of Academic Development 75
Irvine, D. 25
Isocrates 19, 106, 123
Jenkins, A. 70, 78
Johnson, R. 31, 66, 120
Jones, F. 60
Kemmis, S. 39

Kennewick Man 88– 90, 93, 95
Kinman, G. 60
Klein, M. 15
Kroker, A. 92
Kushner, S. 55
Land, R. 75, 121
Language 7–11, 27, 45, 46, 58
Lave, J. 81
League tables 8
Learning
  active 18–20, 23, 30, 55, 69–70, 107, 120
  assessment of 21
  collaborative 38
  digital technology in 121–3
  discovery 105, 108–9
  'deep' *vs* 'surface' 64, 75
  lifelong 28
  outcomes 18–19, 21, 50, 51, 113
  responsibility for 20, 31, 57, 120–2
  student-centred, *see* Learning, active
Learning and Skills Council 7
Lee, M. 88
Leftwich, A. 56
Lenoir, T. 89–90
Levacic, R. 66
Levin 17, 106
Lightfoot, L. 4
London School of Economics (LSE) 93
Love, intellectual 2, 13, 26, 109–116
Luby, A. 55
Lyotard, J-F. 5–6, 13
Macfarlane, B. 12
McIntyre, M. 114
Macnaughton, J. 102
McNay, I. 69
Malcolm, J. 9, 44, 6
Management 67–8, 73, 83–5, 100, 118, 126
Managemerialism 8, 71, 113, 126
  response to 13
Marketization 9, 16, 19, 34–5, 37
  see also Gobalization
Marsh, H. 68, 112
Martin, B. 99
Marton, F. 75
Marxism 96
Maskell, D. 9
Medical humanities 25, 101
Meek, J. 24
Messer-Davidow, E. 23, 94
Metcalfe, J. 6